Straight Parents,
Gay Children

For Better or For Worse® by **Lynn Johnston**

© Lynn Johnston Productions, Inc., Reproduced by permission.

"This book will help to bring Bob's dream of 'an uprising of tens of millions of parents insisting on an end to society's cruelty toward their gay kids' one step closer to reality. Thank you, Bob."

—Candace Gingrich, author of *The Accidental Activist* and associate manager of the National Coming Out Day Project for the Human Rights Campaign

"A penetrating book. . . . With human warmth and insightful anecdotes, Bernstein invites his readers into the intensely emotional, but deeply human, issue of homosexuality. There he discovers light, not darkness, love not fear."

—The Rt. John Shelby Song, Episcopal Bishop, Diocese of Newark, and author of *Living in Sin?: A Bishop Rethinks Human Sexuality*

"If Bob Bernstein's book were compulsory reading in America, the population of bigots would dwindle at a rapid rate. His ability to make the case for fairness and decency in our treatment of each other is unsurpassed."

—Rep. Barney Frank, U.S. House of Representatives (Massachusetts)

"A succinct, moving book about parents who have defied the social stigma of homosexuality to publicly support their gay children."

—*Washington Blade*

"This is a book every parent should read."
—Robb Forman Dew, American Book Award-winning novelist and author of *The Family Heart: A Memoir of When Our Son Came Out*

"Bob Bernstein's invaluable book shows the parents of gay children how to stop merely tolerating their kids and start being their heroes. Is there any higher goal for a parent?"

—Armistead Maupin, author of the *Tales of the City* series

Straight Parents, Gay Children

KEEPING FAMILIES TOGETHER

ROBERT A. BERNSTEIN

THUNDER'S MOUTH PRESS
NEW YORK

Straight Parents Gay Children: Keeping Families Together

Copyright © 1995, 2003 by Robert A. Bernstein
Foreword copyright © 2003 by Betty DeGeneres

Published by
Thunder's Mouth Press

Library of Congress Cataloging-in-Publication Data:

Bernstein, Robert A. (Robert Alen), 1926–
  Straight parents, gay children : keeping families together / by Robert A. Bernstein.
    p. cm.
Includes index.
  ISBN 978-1-56025-452-2
  1. Parents of gays. 2. Homosexuality. 3. Gay men—Family relationships. 4. Lesbians—Family relationships. I. Title.
HQ759.9145 .B47 2003
306.874—dc21
                          2003005226

Book design by Shona McCarthy
Printed in the United States of America
Distributed by Publishers Group West

To the kids: Bobbi,
Donna, Sharon, John,
Dietrich, Allison, Douglas,
Dee Ann

Contents

Acknowledgments

My agent, Frances Goldin, provided me with the initial motivation to write this book and guided the later development of many aspects of it. The encouragement of Neil Ortenberg and Dan O'Connor of Thunder's Mouth Press and Avalon Publishing Group have been important throughout. My daughters' contributions have been invaluable: Sharon's critique of an early draft supplied insights that largely informed the book's eventual shape and substance, and Bobbi served as an unofficial assistant editor of this revision. I am indebted to Avalon editor Michelle Rosenfield for initiating the revision and providing helpful guidance in its completion.

My wife, Myrna, has been a full partner in our journey of enrichment: sharing the adventure of discovery, assisting in interviews, offering penetrating observations, reviewing drafts, and imparting her trademark aura of calm and caring that makes all of my work possible.

Myrna and I are convinced that the ghost of Will Rogers watches over PFLAG meetings: we have never met anyone there we didn't like. And I could not have written this book without the generous and spirited cooperation of scores of PFLAG members and staff workers. Many of these people are mentioned in the book; I wish I had the room to list them all. They have my everlasting thanks.

I have borrowed from two remarkable videos about families with gay members, and I am grateful to their producers. One of them, by Dee Mosbacher and Frances Reid (*Straight from the Heart*, Woman Vision Video, 415-921-5687), 800-343-5440, www.woman-vision.org), was nominated for an Academy Award; the other, by Pam Walton (Gay Youth, Wolfe Video, PO Box 64, Almaden, CA 95042; 408-268-6782, 800-GET-WOLFE, www.wolfevideo.com), is equally insightful.

Foreword

I love this book. If you're a parent whose son or daughter has said those three words to you—no, not "I love you," those other three words, "Mom, I'm gay," or "Dad, I'm gay"—you *need* this book. And if you're the son or daughter who said the three words, I know you'll love it, too.

I've heard of parents who took this news totally in stride. They already had suspicions, or not, but were immediately accepting and understanding. My hat is off to them. It seems that most of us need an adjustment period—a time to refocus, to step back and realize that our children have to live their lives as they were meant to, and not just live out some preconceived idea of what we envision for them.

I'll always be grateful that when Ellen said those three words to me twenty five years ago, she gave me the time I needed to adjust to her surprising news. It is also vital that we kept the lines of communication open. During that time, she wrote me a letter in which she said, ". . . I don't think you'll ever understand." Well, I'm happy to say that I think I have proved her wrong on that one.

In 1997 when Ellen came out publicly, I guess I did, too. I feel privileged to have been the first non-gay spokesperson for the Human Rights Campaign's National Coming Out Project. I've traveled all over the United States, speaking at universities and corporations, speaking out against ignorance and bigotry and speaking for equal rights for our gay sons and daughters.

In the last five and a half years I've been truly blessed with making and keeping many close, dear friends among the gay men and women I've met along the way. I can honestly say that some of the finest people I have ever met in my life are among these gay men and women.

I don't believe a poll has been taken, but here's my own personal finding: among gay men and women is an inordinately large group of overachievers. They can't be "just as good as." They have to be "better than." They have to prove themselves time and again. And they live their lives courageously.

We heterosexuals don't think about this enough—what it would be like to go through life as a contributing, taxpaying, law-abiding, upstanding citizen, yet always knowing in your heart that there are those who despise you without even knowing you. That takes a kind of stamina and bravery that most of us can't even imagine.

That is why *Straight Parents, Gay Children* is so important. If you're a parent who loves all your children unconditionally, you'll recognize yourself in these pages. If a son or daughter has said those three words to you, and you were able to get your priorities in order and not turn off that endless faucet of your love, you'll recognize yourself in these pages.

As parents we must send the message that discrimination against our loved ones is not OK. Our voices must ring out loud and clear and echo throughout the land that hate and bigotry, under any guise, are unacceptable. The stories in this book are representative of thousands upon thousands just like them in families all around the world.

Speak up, folks. Let's make *all* our voices heard.

—Betty DeGeneres

Introduction

I have a gay son, and that's all right with me. What is important is my son the person—his character, his generosity, his talents. His sex life is of no more importance to me than that of his heterosexual brothers and sisters, or of my close friends.

If all parents with gay children could comfortably say "I have a gay child (grandchild, sibling, niece, nephew, cousin, aunt, uncle)," this book would be unnecessary. But millions of parents cannot do this. Some of them are afraid of what others will say. Others are appalled that their children are gay. Still others are ashamed, imagining that something they did caused an effect they have been taught to consider sick and unnatural. And many more are simply unaware, because their gay sons and daughters are afraid to tell them.

Straight Parents, Gay Children can be a great comfort to these millions of parents. Through the collective experience of thousands of families, it reveals that, once over the threshold of misinformation and fear, parents can find liberation in the truth about homosexuality. And this liberation restores and strengthens the natural bonds of love and understanding they have with their sons and daughters.

Parents learn that it is not their children's choice to fall in love with members of their own sex. It is something over which they have no control. The further scientists reach for answers, the greater the conviction that homosexuality is innate, predetermined, fixed. It's neither a defect of moral character nor a failure of will. Some people may consider it blasphemous to call homosexuality an act of God; let us then consider it an act of Nature. Efforts to change that nature, whether cruel or kind, are doomed to failure. Queen Victoria's opinion that women could not be homosexuals did not change any gay person's sexual orientation at the beginning of the century. Neither did Nazi persecution at mid-century. Nor will the present attempts to curb the civil rights of gay people.

There is a great need for the comfort this book can bring to anguished parents by helping them find others like themselves. The most informed estimates place the number of gay Americans at about seventeen million, and almost every gay person has relatives somewhere in this world. Theoretically, there may be seventeen million siblings of gay children, thirty four million parents, sixty eight million grandparents, and so on through other relations. Statistically, all Americans have a reasonably direct stake in understanding homosexuality. Many do not know it because so many gay people keep their sexuality a secret. Many know it but deny or suppress the truth. Others know it, and live in misery fearing the ostracism of society.

When a story about my good relations with my son, Ian, appeared in the *New York Times,* I received many letters from parents of gay children saying how the article had helped them acknowledge the truth. One mother wrote that for years she had suspected her son's secret misery. She later slipped the article under his bedroom door, and a few minutes later he came out—in both senses. There were other letters of greater pain, from young people whose parents had never accepted their homosexuality, and who had disowned them.

Prejudice against homosexuality is deeply rooted in our culture because of religious and psychological legacies difficult to unravel. As with any prejudice, this one runs counter to evidence. President Clinton failed in his intention to repeal the ban on gays in the military because the defense community considered it too disruptive, although most people know that homosexuals have always served, some with great distinction.

No one in this book is advocating special treatment for gay people. What they are advocating is that gay people be treated decently so that their families need not fear to love them, and so that millions of citizens need not fear disgrace, discrimination, and physical assault for their sexual orientation. Relieving the ostracism of gay people everywhere would strengthen family values, no matter what the prevailing political climate may dictate.

Finally, on civil-rights grounds, I don't think it can be put more eloquently than Senator Barry Goldwater has done:

> *The rights and liberties that our founding fathers wrote into the Declaration of Independence and the Constitution were meant for all people. . . . It is time that our nation realized that a significant portion of our society is today excluded and that laws need to be written and enforced to ensure that lesbians and gays are not discriminated against in employment, public accommodations, and housing.*

—Robert MacNeil

She cannot be reduced to statistics, polls, stereotypes, nicknames,
prejudice, opinion.
She is my child.
I still have the same dreams. The details may have changed, but
the dreams are the same.
Of happiness, love, home, family, meaningful work.
Because, you see, she is my child. . . .
She is warm and caring and sensitive and vulnerable and angry
and sad, funny and human.
Yes, she is my child.

—From a poem by Elise Self about her lesbian daughter

1

Rethinking the Unthinkable

My younger daughter, after years of denying to herself that she was gay,* ultimately told the truth to herself, her family, and her personal world. She is one of millions of Americans who increasingly are refusing to live lives of deception, to lie about an important aspect of who they are. And she has thereby led her family down new pathways of understanding.

Telling the truth can set psyches free. It can strengthen family bonds. It can make our society a healthier place. As young people struggle to understand their inner natures, and parents struggle to accept their children's sexuality, honesty and openness are healing ingredients. As society struggles against the sway of ignorance and prejudice, truth, coupled with regard for the dignity and individuality of others, is an indispensable weapon.

---

*Throughout the book, I have used the word gay in a generic sense to refer to both gay men and lesbians, as well as to those who identify as bisexual. For those with transgendered family members, an excellent resource is *Transforming Families* (Oak Knoll Press, 2nd edition, 2003).

This is a book about truth-telling and respect for human differences. It is the story of some extraordinary individuals and a pioneering organization, both of which have demonstrated those qualities' immense potential for good.

Yes, truth-telling can be rewarding. But it can also be difficult and risky. And it is rarely easy.

"How do you feel about having a gay son?"

The question was directed to Paul, sitting with ten or twelve others around a table in a large conference room in a local church. His wife, Marie, had just finished describing her response to their son John's revelation that he was homosexual. She had recounted a persistent, pervasive grief similar to what she had felt when her mother died five years earlier. Periodically, she said, without warning, she was wracked by uncontrollable sobbing. As she spoke, the tears came again.

Across from Paul and Marie, Joan was recovering her composure after telling tearfully how her daughter had come out to her as a lesbian. "I can't imagine what I did wrong," she had said. "Maybe I should have dated more after my divorce, or had more men around the house. . . . Maybe I shouldn't have let her play sports . . . now I can't imagine what sort of terrible life she's going to have."

Paul had come reluctantly, at Marie's urging, and sat stiffly as she sobbed. Now the question to him hung in the air as he looked first at his wife and then turned to the questioner. His response was bitter: "Isn't everybody delighted to have a queer in the family?"

Paul, Marie, and Joan sought assistance from an organization called PFLAG—Parents, Families and Friends of Lesbians and Gays—which among its other activities conducts support groups for distraught parents.

For me and thousands like me, PFLAG has been an invaluable resource. There, parents can rethink the unthinkable, and reclaim the family well-being they thought was irreparably shattered.

Support groups, of course, are not everyone's cup of tea. For many parents, especially fathers, talking openly about some of their deepest feelings does not come easily. But support groups are but one of PFLAG's various activities, and PFLAG in any event is by no means the only valuable resource for parents. A variety of other useful means are available to help parents find their way back to equanimity. (See Appendix for a listing of helpful resources.)

Still, for those who are able to overcome their reluctance to open discussion, the PFLAG payoff can be high-yield. There, typically, our initial distress gradually shades into tolerance and then, for most, unconditional acceptance. There, we can let our anguish hang out, secure in the empathy of those who have experienced the same sense of devastation and loss. We can sense in others the healing qualities of time and understanding. And we soon become closer than ever to our children.

As parents, it turns out, we can learn a lot from our gay kids about such basic matters as personal integrity and respect for individual differences. Legions of us have come to terms with our children's homosexuality and discovered that our lives were not diminished but actually enriched by the process. In this way, PFLAG functions as a sort of alchemist of the soul, converting bereaved parents into active celebrants of openness, integrity and honesty. It leads us gently through the barbed thickets of misguided conventional wisdom and back to where we belong—at our children's sides.

And for many, it is a spur to speak out and tell the world what we have learned about the mindless social prejudice and stereotyping that relegate our loved ones to second-class citizenship. Once-distraught parents find themselves active advocates and educators, challenging the myths and irrational beliefs behind the antigay sentiments that fueled their own initial malaise.

We learn that parents do not "cause" and our children for the most part do not "choose" their sexual orientation. We learn that the much-maligned "lifestyle" of the average gay person is about as lurid as our own, centered on such mundane matters as job, family, friends, home, hobbies, and church. The gay community, it turns out, contains about the same proportion of saints and rascals as any other.

We learn that homosexuality is a lot like left-handedness: a minority but wholly natural and neutral trait that speaks not at all to character or morality. We come to appreciate the courage, sensitivity, and integrity demanded of those who manage, despite society's fierce antagonism, to say simply, "I am what I am."

We learn that the genesis of our distress with our children's gayness is neither our children nor ourselves. It is society's reluctance to renounce archaic myths, superstitions, and hatred. There is nothing "wrong" with our gay children.

But we can't help worrying about them.

For there is something very wrong with a society that irrationally denigrates and discriminates against them. A society that limits their job and housing opportunities. A society that drives gay youth to despair and suicide. A society that too often tacitly encourages the physical violence that is commonly their lot.

It's true that gay Americans enjoy far less hostility than they did when my daughter "came out" to her family more than a decade ago. But while gay teenagers face despair and death for lack of support and role models, the United States remains one of the few remaining developed countries that bans lesbians and gay men from serving openly in the military; the Boy Scouts of America stubbornly insist on violating their own standards of honesty and integrity by expelling outstanding Eagle Scouts for refusing to lie about their same-sex orientation; a hugely popular broadcaster, "Dr. Laura," refers to gays as "deviants" and "pedophiles"; and "You're so gay" remains a devastating put-down in our schools. We are left to wonder whether Dallas voters would react very differently today than they did in 1994 when they overwhelmingly re-elected a judge who had righteously announced he would give the lightest possible sentence to a killer who gunned down, gangster-style, two young gay men.

Gay-bashing appears to serve much the same function that lynching once did: controlling a despised minority through terror. Most antigay violence is not prosecuted, if for no other reason than that the victims do not dare file charges; the publicity could cost them their jobs and their homes. Firing or evicting an employee or tenant simply because he or she is gay remains common.

Slowly, attitudes are changing. An important measure is the fact that by 2003, hundreds of companies were protecting their gay employees by way of antidiscrimination and domestic-partner policies. Of the Fortune 500 companies, for example, more than 60 percent banned discrimination based on sexual orientation, and more than a third offered domestic-partner benefits. Among the hundreds of smaller corporations also doing both of those things was Coors Brewing Company, where the initiative was spearheaded in the 1990s by Mary Cheney, lesbian daughter of Vice President Dick Cheney, and then the company's liaison to the gay community.

Honesty and openness are growing more fashionable. Gays are recognizing the liberating force of coming out of the closet. Their families and friends are learning to distinguish between the realities and myths of homosexuality, and to speak out about their newfound truths.

In these pages, you'll meet some parents who are helping lead the way, others who continue to struggle with what they see as a family disaster, and still others who, however accepting of the realities, remain closeted for fear of endangering their children's livelihood or social well-being. Among those in the first category—genuine pioneers in a cultural revolution—are the following:

- A highly regarded police chief of Portland, Oregon, who changed the culture of a police force and ultimately of an entire city by openly praising and supporting his lesbian daughter—who also happened to be one of his own fine police officers.
- Celebrities such as novelists Stephen King and Anne Rice, Vice President Dick Cheney, television anchor and novelist Robert MacNeil, television critic Gene Shalit, movie stars Cher and Barbra Streisand, and former Senators Barry Goldwater and Claiborne Pell, who have been among the ranks of openly supportive parents of gay children.
- An orthopedic surgeon, fitness buff, and national senior power-lifting champion who told a military board of review, "I wish I could be as good a man as my son"—a former "Top Gun" drummed out of the Navy solely because he was gay.
- A mild-mannered schoolteacher who became the first

parent to parade carrying a sign rallying other parents to support their gay kids.

- A Methodist bishop who simply "knew" that if his own son was gay, the stereotypes had to be wrong, and who has campaigned for decades for increased tolerance within his denomination.
- A Jewish immigrant whose family was decimated by the Holocaust, but who lived to speak—as the mother of a gay child—at the inauguration of the United States Holocaust Memorial Museum on behalf of gay Holocaust victims.

I envision parents such as these as the tip of an iceberg, the visible bit of a potentially millions-strong constituency capable of massive positive social change. By conservative estimate, the number of gay, lesbian, and bisexual Americans is probably about seventeen million. The number of non-gay people who might be expected to be their natural allies—their parents, siblings, cousins, aunts, uncles, grandparents, and close friends—is therefore enormous.

Many of these friends and relatives remain caught up in society's prevailing mood of intolerance. But I am convinced that many of them are now silent simply because they are unaware that their silence helps perpetuate the oppression of those they love. They do not realize that they themselves have the power to end that injustice by speaking out against it.

I believe that parents, families, and friends of gays will be in the vanguard of any meaningful breakthrough to the soul of America. We speak to the mainstream *from* the mainstream. We wield the clout of sheer numbers. We are—potentially—a powerful army for social good.

But our ranks are now missing millions of troops who do not realize how desperately they are needed in the trenches.

But of course, I was not aware of any of these matters when my daughter broke the news that too often can destroy a family—but made ours, as so many others, stronger in the long run.

2

Our Family Digests the News

In the play *Twilight of the Golds*, the mother of a gay son tells him, "I must have dressed you funny." The line inevitably draws a hearty laugh, as theatergoers intuitively grasp the nature of the trauma that parents typically experience when they learn they have a gay child. The revelation can trigger outrageous, even ludicrous, guilt. In our own family, as we shall see, my daughter Bobbi recalls her mother wondering in passing whether she was at fault for marrying a man—me—shorter than herself!

Guilt is just one of a range of inner torments a child's coming out may arouse in parents. In general, our family was relatively lucky, for reasons I go into below, to be spared much of the devastation that often tears families apart when they learn they have a gay member. But it's no mystery why the disclosure can wreak havoc. Many, if not most, Americans simply assume that homosexuals are sinful or sick—unsavory outcasts on a lonely, noxious fringe of society.

The assumption is not only largely untrue. It is classic irony.

Scores of history's most creative, influential, and inspiring humans have had significant same-sex relationships. They include philosophers (e.g., Socrates and Plato), rulers (e.g., Alexander the Great and Peter the Great), artists (e.g., da Vinci and Michelangelo), poets (e.g., Byron and Whitman), novelists (e.g., Hans Christian Andersen and Virginia Woolf), dramatists (e.g., Marlowe and Wilde), composers (e.g., Tchaikovsky and Copland), social activists (e.g., Susan B. Anthony and Jane Addams); economists (e.g., Sir John Maynard Keynes), and an endless list of theatrical and entertainment standouts. A complete list would fill many pages—despite the fact that any such compilation virtually by definition can only skim the surface, since legions of past gay greats were themselves painstakingly closeted, and so shall ever remain.

In contemporary society, with societal bias slowly easing, more of our current celebrities are "coming out" each year. They include stars of virtually every field, including religion, sports, journalism, business, and, not surprisingly, the arts and theater. As of this writing, Congress has had five openly gay members, and throughout the country, hundreds of openly gay public servants hold posts as state judges, legislators, and mayors, as well as with city and county councils, school boards, and miscellaneous offices such as sheriff and recorder of deeds. (For more details, see Chapter 11.)

Tellingly, gay Americans were among the heroes on our national watershed day, September 11, 2001. Mark Kendall Bingham, an openly gay man, was one of the "Let's Roll" group of passengers who wrested control of a hijacked plane headed for the U.S. capital and caused it to crash in Pennsylvania; at Bingham's memorial service, Senator John McCain movingly acknowledged that "I may very well owe my life to Mark." Among those buried alive in the World Trade Center rubble was the Reverend Mychal Judge, a gay Franciscan and fire department chaplain, who died while ministering to his firefighters.

These considerations make an important commentary on common stereotypes. In fact, gays always have and presumably always will represent prominent, rich threads in the tapestry of civilized life.

I personally have met hundreds of lesbians and gay men whose lives would make any parent proud. Some are professionals—competent and respected physicians, lawyers, architects, professors, artists, authors, and so on. Others are memorable because of highly attractive personal characteristics: compassion, humor, imagination, talent. Many are in long-term, life-enhancing relationships and living productive and rewarding lives. They evoke affection and respect. My life is richer for knowing them.

Of course, like most parents who learn a child is gay, I was wholly unaware of such matters when Bobbi was growing up. Nor, more importantly, did Bobbi know these things. For her, as for all teenagers of her era—and virtually all today—she had to come to grips with her gayness in a social environment that amounted to a hostile wilderness dotted with emotional land mines. (See chapter 5, "Growing Up Gay.") She emerged relatively unscathed and is now a successful attorney. But she did it without the aid of the parental or community support to which all teenagers ideally are entitled, and her successful passage is a tribute both to her courage and her good fortune.

An overriding regret for me—and for many parents I have since met—is that her mother, stepmother, and I could not help her when she needed us most. I like to think that we could have spared her years of inner terror and doubt; that we would have given her the time and emotional space to discover for herself, without fear or panic, the nature of her sexual identity; that we would have assured her that whatever her orientation might be, it would never diminish either her worth as a person or our own love for her.

I like to think this would have been the case, but I cannot be totally confident of it. For when Bobbi was a teenager struggling to find her place in the world, her mother, stepmother, and I were still relatively conventionally minded members of the homophobic mainstream. Could we have responded with understanding, acceptance, and patience? I don't know, and the answer is now irrelevant. Only after years of her lonely inner struggle with her identity would she describe it to us.

Bobbi's principal weapon in her struggle to quell her unwanted feelings was denial. Before high school, she had fleeting crushes on other girls, but gave them no particular thought. Then, one day in high school, she found herself thinking about another girl, "She's really sexy," but the feeling was unacceptable. "You didn't think that," she told herself. "Forget that." And for the most part, she did manage to ignore and repress such feelings. But the occasional thought that she might be gay triggered spasms of terror.

Bright, talented, extroverted, and a standout athlete, Bobbi made friends easily. She dated a number of boys, and formed lasting (but passionless) friendships with at least two of them. Dating reinforced her denial and seemed to make the threat of her deeper stirrings more remote. By her senior year, she was aware that she wanted a boyfriend so that other people wouldn't think she was gay, but she was still denying the possibility to herself. To maintain her belief, she had to resort to some offbeat logic: since her attraction to women was different from her attraction to men, the former was not sexual and therefore did not mean she was gay. But mental gymnastics would not long stem the mounting inner pressures.

After high school, she enrolled at Stanford, where she met a number of openly homosexual students in a relatively gay-friendly climate. Nevertheless, her self-denial and its accompanying anxiety continued to grow during her first year. Secretly, she had fallen in love with her roommate, Jill, and that terrified her. She even turned to religion, until then a matter of indifference to her. Her religious background had been haphazard: she had attended occasional Protestant services with her mother, and had sometimes come to my Unitarian church when staying with me. Now, however, she seriously considered embracing Catholicism. She thought that if she went to church often enough, if she prayed hard enough, perhaps her dreaded feelings would go away. Three or four times a day, she intoned the standard Hail Mary and Lord's Prayer, capped by the plea, "Please, God, don't let me be gay." Only later would she learn that such frantic pleas to God are common among gay adolescents.

As she strained to prove to herself that she was "normal," Bobbi continued to date young men. Early in her sophomore year, she began to see Michael, a handsome, charming classmate. When she came home for Christmas vacation and people asked about Michael, she heard herself describing someone she clearly thought was wonderful. She told her friends, in all sincerity, that he was probably the most brilliant and talented person she had ever met—"And yeah, he's really cute."

Everybody assumed she was in love. And she couldn't explain even to herself why she *wasn't* in love. Then, during that vacation, she met Sasha, whom she knew to be lesbian and whom she thought was a "dashingly beautiful woman." They spent some time together, did a lot of talking, and a close friendship bloomed. Bobbi found herself thinking more and more about Sasha.

On the plane back to school, she realized that she was dreading seeing Michael, and at first wondered why. Then, suddenly, the likelihood that she was gay burst through her wall of denial and into her consciousness.

She wrote to Sasha, baring her distress, and got back ten pages of sound advice: If you're gay that's fine, or if you're not, that's fine; but if you are, and really care about Michael, then you should be fair and release him. Bobbi accepted the wisdom. The news might hurt Michael for a while, but he was a good friend and she owed him honesty. He would get over it and find somebody who could love him the way he needed to be loved.

So she went to Michael's room and sat on the floor, her back to him as he sat on the edge of a chair, to tell him all. But for some minutes, she could only mumble incoherently. (Michael later said that the severity of her distress had led him to believe she was trying to tell him either that she was dying or sleeping with his best friend.) Finally, she spit it out: "Michael, I think I might be gay."

Michael was silent for what seemed to Bobbi an eternity. Then he took her hand and said, "I know this is a hard time for you. I want you to know that whatever you ultimately decide, I'm here for you." At that, Bobbi burst into tears, they hugged, and they talked until four in the morning.

Now, with no secrets between them, their friendship and their comfort with each other grew. Sasha came to visit Bobbi, and Michael spent pleasant hours with the two of them.

Bobbi did not immediately come out to all of her friends. So, ironically, the relaxed affability between Bobbi and Michael and their open affection led many on campus to assume they were an item. But of course

Michael wanted to see other women, and one of them was a friend of Bobbi's. When Michael approached her, the friend was indignant: "How can you do this to Bobbi!" To rescue Michael, Bobbi was forced to come out to her friend sooner than she otherwise would have.

Soon she had told all her friends. Spontaneously—almost magically—the oppression and terror so long her constant companions evaporated.

Coming out to roommate Jill, who called Bobbi by the affectionate nickname "Dudie," was difficult, even though the tension between them had eased to some extent after Bobbi had come out to herself and started dating another campus lesbian. As Bobbi stammered and hesitated, Jill—who said she "pretty much knew" what Bobbi was trying to say—asked her, "Is there anything I can say to make this easier?" Bobbi then just blurted it out: "I'm gay." And Jill responded, "That's cool, Dudie."

Two years later, the *Stanford Daily* would run a front-page story about Jill and Bobbi, captioned "Best Friends." With it was a picture of the two, still roommates, posing affectionately outside their dormitory behind chalked symbols on the courtyard cement depicting their respective sexual orientations. Still more years later, Jill, by then a professional actress, would do a reading at Bobbi's commitment ceremony with her life partner, and Bobbi would return the compliment (sans stage training) at Jill's wedding.

But that gets ahead of the story.

Once Bobbi was out on campus, life as an openly lesbian woman presented new challenges. Among the first was coming out to her family.

Bobbi had no assurances as to what her family's reaction might be. But she had been warned by older gays of some of the common parental reactions. At the extreme, it was then common—and today is still not at all unusual—for teens to be beaten, disowned, or thrown out on the street. Even among those who truly love their gay children, the typical parent passes through a painful range of emotions, from shock, disbelief, and guilt to denial, anger, and depression.

For many, the process is quite similar to mourning the loss of a family member. In a way, they do experience a type of death—that of a set of important parental images and expectations, including visions of grandchildren and of a respectable and respected future for the child. In the shock of the parents' first reaction, the child of their cherished images seems no longer to exist.

Healing, as after an actual death, proceeds at different paces for different people, moving painfully through the various stages of grief before arriving, for most, at acceptance. But unlike the death of a loved one, this trauma can't be freely shared. Friends and neighbors don't bear food and solace to the family hearth. (God forbid they should even know!) Society provides no comforting rituals, no funerals or wakes.

Why are we so disturbed by homosexuality? The reasons are complex. Part of the answer is simply the ageless human distrust of those who are "different," the same reaction that seems to underlie so much prejudice against those of different race, gender, and so on. But this difference has to do with sex, and that's an aspect of human nature that has generated more taboos, confusion, fears, and repression than any other.

So the emotional pressure-cooker in this instance projects some unusually vicious images, for which "deviant," "pervert," and "pedophile" are some of the generally accepted labels. And once programmed, as with other cultural prejudices, these images are reinforced by daily input from ordinary conversation, jokes, and the media. The drumbeat of negativity, moreover, creates the perception that sex is the defining aspect of homosexuals. They are not people who work, worship, tend their gardens, love their families, shop for groceries. They are sex-obsessed "sodomites."

Homosexuality also threatens traditional gender roles. So gay men are ridiculed as "pansies," too effeminate to be respected as "real" men. Lesbians are seen as man-hating "bull dykes," too unfeeling to assume their "proper" roles of dependency on men. And "traditional family values" becomes a catchphrase sufficient in itself to convey the supposed social threat of homosexuality. For the truly "traditional" family is of course one in which gender roles are clear: male as head of the clan, female as servile homemaker.

All of this psychic unrest is handily rationalized into an unexamined assumption that gay people are sick or sinful or both. (See Chapter 5.) So it is hardly surprising that a child's coming out can be such a devastating blow to the unsuspecting parent.

When Bobbi came out to her family, her mother, Carol, and I had been divorced for some years. Carol's reaction was largely typical. When Bobbi spoke the fateful words, "I'm gay," Carol first tried to pass it off as a joke. "That's not funny," she said. When she realized Bobbi was serious, she said Bobbi must be mistaken: "You haven't really given boys a try." Then guilt and grief descended upon her, and became her overriding emotions for the next several months.

Like the mother in *Twilight of the Golds*, Carol castigated herself with a litany of self-blame. She had not been caring enough. She shouldn't have let Bobbi play sports. She should have remarried so that Bobbi would always have had "a man around the house." (Carol and I separated when Bobbi was seven.) She shouldn't have allowed Bobbi to attend a "liberal" college. She shouldn't have agreed to giving Bobbi a name that sounds like a boy's. Or even (as Bobbi insists Carol once remarked) she should have married someone taller than herself.

Out of the blue, she would be overcome by despondency and break into tears, even when she hadn't been thinking of Bobbi. She envisioned a life of loneliness and desolation for her daughter. And she found herself largely unable to share her anguish with friends.

I had the good fortune to be spared much of the grief Carol was experiencing. As a young man, my attitude toward homosexuality had been conventionally, and I now believe shamefully, hateful. I remember I was proud to be friends with a college fraternity brother who was a gay-basher. A tall, muscular boy, though ordinarily of easygoing nature, he was driven by some compelling malice to attack the few open homosexuals he encountered in off-campus nightspots. His high moral dudgeon and its savage expression were greatly admired by the "brothers." And I was among the admirers.

The intervening years, however, had seen a change of perspective.

At first, I suppose my attitude toward homosexuality was similar to that of most heterosexual adult males—largely an indifference toward something that seemed sufficiently disgusting to be unworthy of serious thought.

In retrospect, I now realize—an awareness that must always have been lurking in some hidden recess of reluctant consciousness—that various of my professional colleagues have been gay. I recall, for example, attending the quite elaborate wedding and reception of a young colleague whose cohabitation with his wife, for reasons never divulged, rather amazingly ended only two days later; and with my enhanced hindsight I now realize that his friendship with several young men had always seemed inordinately close. To my knowledge, he never married again and I later learned that in the community to which he subsequently moved his professional practice, he was generally considered "one of those." But during the years I served with him as a colleague— and, I thought, rather close friend—no such suspicion ever entered my conscious mind.

I recall two events that contributed to a subtle softening of my harsh undergraduate views.

The first occurred during a series of interviews I happened to be doing with a prisoner at a Texas state prison who told me he was gay. I said I wasn't surprised, since it was my understanding that homosexuality was common among prisoners deprived of female companionship. "No, you don't understand," he said. "Those guys' sexual fantasies are about women. Mine are about men." His simple statement was something of a revelation: at its core, I realized, homosexuality wasn't about behavior, it was about a state of being that spoke to one's deepest inner feelings and personal identity.

Another milestone for me was an adult class on sexuality in which I had enrolled as a matter of curiosity when Bobbi was about seven. There, in an environment of total openness with other adults of both sexes, I found myself one of the ardently heterosexual males who nonetheless confessed to long-standing, till-then-unspoken fears of potential latent homosexuality. This anxiety, we decided, had nothing in fact to do with homosexuality. Rather, it reflected some deep-seated insecurity about our manhood, our "machismo," as so often culturally defined. Perhaps more importantly, the experience of open discussion about sexuality led to the inevitable realization that each of us was as individual, as unique, in our sexual feelings and experiences as in any other aspect of our lives and personalities. More comfortable, as a result, with my own sexuality, I found it easier to be comfortable with that of others, however different from my own.

And my timing proved to be fortunate. For when Bobbi was still only nine or ten, I began to wonder—the thoughts triggered by her "boyish" mannerisms and "tomboy" interests—whether she might be gay. (When she was eight, she told me she wanted to play football. I told her—as she has never let me forget—that "girls don't play football." She would, in fact, in defiance of paternal wisdom, shortly be holding her own with boys in football games in the park.)

It would be another decade or so before she would admit her homosexuality to herself. But meanwhile, my suspicions—however rooted in simple stereotypical thinking—served me well. At least I was *thinking* about a matter that forced me to confront my own residue of unease about homosexuality.

At first I was dismayed by the thought that my darling little girl might be one of "them." (I had no such concerns, for similarly stereotypical reasons, about my equally darling but more "feminine" older daughter, Sharon.) I was able to express my fears to Myrna, to whom I was then engaged; we discussed the matter often in ensuing years. Bits of genuine evidence did emerge, such as Bobbi's utter lack of adolescent excitement toward the attractive boys she dated as a teenager. By the time of her ultimate disclosure, we were sufficiently prepared to avoid panic or shout disapproval. We were far from understanding all the personal and social ramifications of Bobbi's disclosure. But at least we could assure her that her gayness did not diminish our love for her.

Myrna and I were fortunate. We had adjusted gradually to information that usually strikes unwary parents with mind-blowing impact. We had acknowledged the reality that, gay or not, Bobbi would remain the same accomplished and gracious young woman who, like my other daughter and Myrna's two sons, made us proud. We now simply had an additional piece of information about Bobbi. To be sure, it was information that in our moral bookkeeping we at first automatically entered in the debit column. But we didn't expect any of our children to be perfect. And if being gay was to us a fairly substantial liability—well, Bobbi's numerous assets still, for us, struck a clear balance in the black.

Bobbi came out to Myrna and me on a summer evening in 1987, between her sophomore and junior years at Stanford. She was shocked by our lack of surprise or distress. But if we were not surprised, we were nevertheless enlightened. Her story afforded us our first glimpse into the extraordinary process of coming out. (The phrase of course is shorthand for "coming out of the closet," and refers to the acknowledgment of one's same-sex orientation to oneself and to others.) We began to realize that it involves much more than mere declaration; rather, it is an inner dynamic, a journey of struggle and growth. It is a profound human experience, reflecting the ageless human striving for personal integrity. It is the effort to find and embrace one's authentic self—to say, "I am what I am, and that's OK"—in the face of a hostile society that inundates gay youth with shame. In effect, coming out represents liberation from hand-me-down "truths"—the powerful "shoulds" and "must nots" of encrusted social norms—that, unexamined, can produce a type of emotional bondage.

Myrna and I were not then aware of the full impact that Bobbi's coming out would have on our own lives. But we were fascinated and

21

impressed by the story she told us that night—and in particular by the tender maturity of her relationship with Michael.

Afterward, I lay in bed processing what Bobbi had told us. My respect for my daughter was enhanced by the events she had related. If her homosexuality reflected something "wrong" with her, I thought, there was nevertheless something right about the way she was dealing with it. I could only applaud her rigorous honesty with herself and with those to whom she was close, such as Michael and her own family.

The next morning, on my old-fashioned office typewriter, I wrote her a letter now permanently pasted—worn-ribbon type, cross-outs, typos, and all—in her personal scrapbook. In it, I expressed my pride in her personal integrity and sensitivity in dealing with others. The nature of her sexual orientation, I said, obviously had no bearing in itself on her inherent decency as a human being, so tellingly demonstrated in the way she had managed her relationships with Jill and Michael. "I guess what all this boils down to," I concluded, "is that you have given me even more reason for the love and respect I have always felt for you. Thanks."

Nine years later, I would read portions of the letter on an "Oprah Winfrey Show" segment dealing with gay issues. And two years still later, Michael would travel cross-country, together with Jill and a dozen or so other Stanford friends, to join more than a hundred family members and friends at Bobbi's moving commitment ceremony with her life partner, Donna Hylton.

One day shortly after Bobbi's coming out, Carol and I had lunch. She was still in shock, envisioning a bleak, loveless life for Bobbi. I didn't think that had to be the case, but I had no real evidence to support my assurances.

However, I did come up with an idea that not only helped Carol adjust but set my own life on a new course of discovery and enrichment.

I recalled having seen notices in my church bulletin about meetings of a group called Parents and Friends of Lesbians and Gays. (*Families* wasn't added to PFLAG's name until 1993.) In my ignorance, I told Carol it was part of the church program; only later did I learn that PFLAG was an international organization whose local chapter just happened to meet in our church. I said that Myrna and I would accompany Carol if she wanted to go to a meeting. Carol agreed.

So it was that a few weeks later my wife, my ex-wife, and I attended our first PFLAG meeting. Like the evening of Bobbi's coming out, the meeting for me proved to be a moving experience that hinted at new horizons of awareness.

The facilitator of the meeting, Paulette Goodman, was a prototypical grandmother, short and full-bodied, with kindly eyes smiling through thick rimless eyeglasses. She spoke with a mild French accent in soft tones that were nonetheless precise and compelling. She would later become widely known during her four-year tenure as PFLAG's national president, when her influence would extend into the White House itself. (Her story is told in Chapter 12.) At the moment, as she informed the group, she was both the local chapter president and Mid-Atlantic regional director of PFLAG. She described the organization as dedicated to the support and education of parents, but also to helping create a better society for those she referred to as "our gay loved ones."

For some reason, I found the latter phrase particularly compelling. It suggested that at PFLAG, the term gay would not be used to connote perversion and deviance, but to refer to precious, valued family members. It suggested there were numerous others with gay children like Bobbi, whom they considered to be fine, worthwhile human beings.

The group included five or six gay and lesbian people. One was a handsome young man, tall, blond, blue-eyed—in appearance and manner a young woman's classic heartthrob. Bob worked as a bank teller and was majoring in finance as a part-time university student; he wanted to come out to his midwestern parents but feared their reaction, particularly his father's.

Lisa was a schoolteacher, and in a committed relationship with a young woman with whom she lived. She loved her job, but was terrified that school authorities might discover she was a lesbian. She had come out to her parents some months earlier. So far, she said, they were "not very good about it"; she was hoping to persuade them to attend a PFLAG meeting near their home in the South.

Pete, a professional who would become a friend of ours, told us he had been married and had an eight-year-old daughter. He and his wife had divorced when he could no longer deny his gayness to himself or her, but he had maintained a close relationship with his daughter. At the moment, she was at the zoo with Pete's life companion, a lawyer, whom she fondly called "Uncle Steve"; she was staying with Pete and Steve for the weekend, as she did regularly under Pete's visitation arrangements. (When the meeting was over, we met Steve and the happy little girl, when they arrived to pick up her father.) Pete attended PFLAG meetings, he said, to help assure parents that their gay sons could live stable, happy lives.

Among the parents were Veronica and Jerry Colfer, both seventy-eight, who, like us, were attending their first meeting. They had known for fourteen years that their son was gay and had long since come to full acceptance. Nevertheless, as devout Catholics, they had fearfully refrained from discussing the matter with friends or fellow parishioners. After years of closeted discomfort, they took obvious relief in being able to speak freely about their love for their son Paul and his lover, Tom. They were there in part because the pressure to reveal their situation to others had increased: Tom had AIDS. The Colfers referred to Tom as their "son-in-love," a term fondly used (with its counterpart, "daughter-in-love") by PFLAG parents.

When it was her turn to speak, Carol expressed her misgivings at some length, weeping openly at one point. Gently, Paulette and others assured her that her feelings were common to "new parents" (another PFLAG term). Their empathy and understanding provided immediate relief, and her "recovery" moved rapidly from that point.

I had long taken a certain pride in being what I considered progressive and open-minded. But as I listened to the young gay people, I could not deny my sense of surprise that they seemed not to fit the stereotypes in my mind. And as I listened to Paulette and some of the "old parents," I realized how ignorant I was of a matter on which I no longer had any right to be uninformed.

Paulette might have been addressing me when she gently but firmly corrected a mother who suggested her gay son was not normal. Just because they comprise a minority, Paulette said, homosexual people are no less normal than other minorities, such as, for example, those who are left-handed. Societies throughout history have had approximately the same proportion of homosexual persons, she said; some of the most illustrious figures of history have been gay, and some cultures, such as those of Native Americans, have reserved special places of honor for their gay members.

I was moved by what I was hearing. Perhaps, after all, I thought, there was nothing wrong with the daughter I respected so deeply. Perhaps *whom* she loved was not as important as the fact that she was capable of loving. Perhaps "gay loved one" was not necessarily an oxymoron.

Among her announcements that day, Paulette told us of a national gay and lesbian march on Washington scheduled for some weeks later. Neither Carol nor I had ever taken part in any sort of political demonstration. But we both lived in the suburbs of Washington and decided to go, since it seemed a relatively simple way of demonstrating support for Bobbi (who was already back at Stanford).

Myrna decided not to accompany us. Keenly aware of the prevalence of antigay sentiments, Myrna was beset by scary visions of ugly confrontations created by parade protesters. So she wished Carol and me well—but no thanks, she'd stay home. After hearing about our experience, she regretted her decision, and now enjoys marching with PFLAG in similar parades.

October 11, 1987, was a crisp, sunny day in the nation's capital. Carol and I stood for more than an hour with our relatively tiny delegation of parents—a grizzled crew of maybe 150, virtually lost in a sea of some 600,000, mostly young, people thronging Memorial Mall. But we were surprised to see banners indicating that parents had come from as far away as California, Colorado, and Washington State. Some carried signs with simple messages of support, such as "We love our gay and lesbian children." Finally, at a signal from parade marshals, we began a slow march through the Ellipse and onto Seventeenth Street. From there the throng would walk the short block to Pennsylvania Avenue and turn right, past the White House and toward Capitol Hill.

We hadn't taken more than twenty-five steps when we began to hear a low rumble that, to Carol and me, seemed ominous. Already a little edgy in this unfamiliar setting, we glanced at each other apprehensively. Gay-rights marches, after all, were for us hardly common fare. Our confusion and unease heightened as the sound grew in volume.

Then, as we looked around us, we understood what we were hearing. The rumble was actually a growing roar of welcome from the massive throng, directed to our little band! It crescendoed into a deafening ovation that followed us up Seventeenth Street and all the way along Pennsylvania Avenue. For us, the march became a blur of excited faces, shouting voices, and waves of wild applause. Many of the faces were streaked with tears. Youths ran sobbing from the curbside to hug us, crying, "I wish my parents were here." Others with cameras swarmed about us, eager to preserve the memory of our symbolic presence.

Plainly, the thunder and the tears were welling up out of a vast void in the hearts of these young people. By their tumultuous ovation, they were telling us how profoundly they longed for the acceptance and support of their own families.

Soon, we too were in tears. In part, ours were tears of pleasure and gratitude for the stirring welcome. But they were also tears of sorrow for the personal anguish that obviously fueled this powerful response. They were tears of regret for millions of families throughout the country that had been senselessly torn apart and were in desperate need of help. It was a searing personal experience that would leave an indelible mark on each of us.

That night, as on the night Bobbi came out to us, I lay in bed reviewing a life-changing experience. I thought about how parents like myself, joined together in sufficiently large numbers, could stem the tide of tragedy I had sensed that afternoon. And I pledged myself to the mission of fighting the deadly prejudice that threatened the well-being, and sometimes the very lives, of our gay kids.

Four months later I described my newfound commitment in a *New York Times* column that was reprinted widely around the country. "My daughter is a lesbian," I wrote. "She also is the light of my life, a talented young woman whose joyous spirit helps brighten the lives of others." I wrote of the soul-shaking experience of the march on Washington. I told of my vision of a day when parents by the millions would enlist in the crusade for their gay kids' dignity. I pleaded the cause of "the most basic of freedoms: the right to be what one is."

The day the column appeared, my office telephone hardly stopped ringing. Most of the calls were from young gay people wanting to thank me personally. (They even included two former members of the highest legal office in the land, the office of the Solicitor General of the United States.)

The onetime admirer of a gay-basher had become a brazen booster of equality for homosexual citizens. But I still had a lot to learn about the legions of inspiring, courageous parents and young people I would be joining in a crusade against ignorance and apathy; about some darker sides of well-meaning social and religious traditions; and about the self-defeating forces of righteous extremism that in the name of a loving God can, however well-intentioned, tear families asunder.

3

Families Fighting the Myths

"It is clear that heterosexual prejudice against homosexuals must take its place alongside witchcraft, slavery, and other ignorant beliefs and oppressive institutions that we have abandoned."

So writes Episcopal Bishop (retired) John Shelby Spong. And indeed, parents' principal problem on learning they have a gay child is overcoming those "ignorant beliefs"—the myths so important in shaping our preconceptions.

If you're reading this book, there's not much chance you're like Lyn's mother, who committed her lesbian daughter to a mental hospital, or like Matthew's father, who threw his gay son bodily out of the house. (See Chapter 5, "Growing Up Gay.") Your reaction to having a gay child is probably more like that of a friend of mine, I'll call him Jim.

Jim was one of the early white civil-rights activists. Nearly half a century ago, he and his wife purchased a home in a planned integrated community composed of roughly half whites and half Negroes, as African-Americans were then called. There, they raised three children, a boy and two girls, who grew up essentially indifferent to the skin colors of their neighborhood playmates.

So it should have come as no surprise, much less shock, when one of his daughters, Ann, started dating a black boy. But shocked—and heartily disapproving—Jim was. "My intellectual beliefs were out of sync with my guts," he says. "I, the great interracial pioneer of the integrated tract!" Then his second daughter, Beth, brought home her life partner—another woman—and Jim discovered another, deeper layer of prejudice. "I had raised hell about Ann having a black boyfriend," he says. "But, boy, then I wished Beth had done the same thing."

Jim doesn't think homosexuality is "wrong," any more than he thinks racism is right, and he fully accepts and supports Beth and her life partner. Still, he says feelingly, "I wish with all my heart that Beth was straight."

Among parents who genuinely love their children, Jim's reaction is classic, although the clarity of his insight into his ambivalence—that his "beliefs and guts are out of sync"—is perhaps unusual. But like him, millions of parents continue to love and support their gay children while grappling with varying degrees of discomfort.

Prejudice runs deep, in defiance of reason or objective reality. And homophobia, the bias born of fear and hatred of gays, perhaps runs even deeper than most. To be sure, the gay community, like any other, has its share of psychological and moral misfits. But the conventional wisdom that being gay in itself means being sick or sinful, or somehow dangerous to others or to society as a whole, is a groundless fabrication.

In this chapter, we first consider in turn each of the myths—sickness, sin, and the attendant notion that homosexuality is a "choice"—that continue to plague parents. Then, we look at the havoc created in five families when the now-regretful parents made the mistake of acting on their ingrained mythical beliefs.

The medical profession for years dealt with homosexuality as a personality disorder. The notion was fueled by early studies that looked only at gay men who had sought psychological counseling. The logic therefore was based on a glaring non sequitur—since gay patients who sought psychiatric help were maladjusted, all gays must be maladjusted.

Every relevant professional organization—among them, the American Medical Association, American Psychological Association, American Psychiatric Association, American Association of Psychoanalysts, and the American Academy of Pediatrics—now recognizes the fallacy of the "sickness" myths. The misguided notions are nevertheless still given credence by many nonprofessionals. Perhaps the most widespread misconception is that gayness stems from an unhealthy home environment—the most popular villains being a dominant, smothering mother and a passive or indifferent father. For years, many psychiatrists talked seriously about a "homosexual personality" that classified gays as vindictive and aggressive, unable to sustain healthy relationships. All such theories have been thoroughly discredited.

Dr. Evelyn Hooker, a research psychologist, was the first to point out the anomaly of judging all homosexuals by samples limited to those under psychological treatment. A heterosexual with numerous gay friends, Hooker was struck by the discrepancy between prevailing medical views and her friends' robust mental health. So she undertook her own government-funded study in 1957, applying intensive personality testing to a random group of gays and a matched group of non-gays. The study's case files, including all the standard diagnostic psychological profiles, were analyzed by a panel of psychiatrists, who had of course been trained to believe that to be gay was to be mentally ill. Nonetheless, they were unable to distinguish gays from non-gays. The results stunned the psychological world.

Sixteen years later, in 1973, the American Psychiatric Association (APA) finally got around to removing homosexuality from its list of disorders. In doing so, the APA stated that there was no reason why a lesbian or gay man couldn't be just as healthy, effective, law-abiding, and productive as any heterosexual. Other professional groups, as noted above, soon followed suit.

Hooker, who died in 1996, saw the notion of homosexuality as illness as simply a reflection of social norms. She liked to compare it to what was once diagnosed to be a psychological maladjustment among slaves—their symptom was running away from the plantation!

No less irrational—but perhaps even more profoundly ingrained in the social consciousness—is the widespread view that homosexuality is sinful. Most major American religious denominations are now essentially split down the middle, with a formidable faction still convinced of that "truth." Only a few of the major mainstream denominations— notably the United Church of Christ, Unitarian-Universalism, and Reform Judaism—formally approve of ordaining openly gay ministers or rabbis, and only a minority of American clergy will conduct same-sex ceremonies of union. (By contrast, gay marriage is now legal in the Netherlands and Belgium; the parliament of the European Union has voted to recognize such marriages and gay registered partnerships across national borders; and the state of Vermont in 2000 became the first in the United States to grant legal rights to resident gay and lesbian couples that are essentially equivalent to those of married heterosexuals.)

Normally, the Bible is cited as the ultimate justification for unequivocal condemnation of homosexuality. In fact, however, the Good Book is ambiguous on the subject. Consider, for example, the famous story of Sodom and Gomorrah, from which the word *sodomy* comes and which undergirds much of the religion-based denunciation of gays as "sodomites." In the view of most serious biblical scholars, the actual targets of the passage are inhospitality and indifference to the poor. Peter J. Gomes, professor of Christian morals at Harvard, has written, "To suggest that Sodom and Gomorrah is about homosexual sex is an analysis of about as much worth as suggesting that the story of Jonah and the whale is a treatise on fishing."

The most explicit biblical condemnation of homosexuality is in Leviticus, where it is labeled an "abomination." But the same book also proscribes such matters as wearing garments with two different kinds of yarn, planting two different kinds of seed in the same field, eating raw meat, and touching the skin of a dead pig. So to be consistent, people who quote Leviticus to condemn homosexuality should among other things avoid playing football—or for that matter any sport, if it means wearing a polyester-cotton blend uniform or warm-up suit.

As for the New Testament, there is no indication that Jesus ever mentioned homosexuals or homosexuality. He simply related a message of love, charity, and acceptance of all of God's creatures. Passages seemingly negative to homosexuality derive from Paul, but many biblical scholars see these primarily as proscriptions against what might be called "unnaturalness." While it is natural for a heterosexual to make love to someone of the opposite sex, the same act is quite unnatural for a lesbian or gay man. And can there in any event be anything more natural, whatever the gender of the partners, than a sincere love that contributes to a couple's growth and fullness-of-being?

Despite this shaky biblical basis, homosexuality has long been assumed to be a sin, an unquestioned evil in the same way murder, rape, and incest were. Only now—and only with severe attendant social upheaval—is the notion giving way. We are learning that same-sex attraction, while a distinct minority trait, is no less natural, for example, than left-handedness, which interestingly occurs at about the same rate.

There is no reputable scientific evidence suggesting that sexual orientation is anything other than an innate, inseparable element of the personal identity of every human being.

Research strongly suggests that homosexuality might have a significant genetic component, and in any event is strongly influenced by biochemical events prior to birth. In 1991, a Salk Institute neuroscientist, Dr. Simon LeVay, found striking differences in the brain anatomy of gay and non-gay men. The same year, a study of twins found a significantly higher correlation of sexual orientation between identical as opposed to fraternal twins. In 1993, Dr. Dean Hamer of the National Institutes of Health discovered a likely genetic link to homosexuality in the X chromosome, although a later Canadian study cast some doubt on those results. In 1994, two Canadian researchers even found a statistically significant difference in fingerprint patterns, which develop in the fetus, between groups of gay and heterosexual males.

Interestingly, studies have even found evidence of homosexuality among fruit flies and sheep, including some indication that the prevalence among male sheep is roughly the same as among human males.

Research teams from Northwestern University, Boston University, and Johns Hopkins University have all found evidence of genetic factors in homosexuality, and they agree that sexual orientation is in any event fixed by the first few years of life.

In the final analysis, what "causes" homosexuality would seem to be unimportant. The salient fact is that it does exist, and the vast majority of gay people—the same as straight people—will tell you that their orientation is an innate, unchangeable part of who they are. For some, the orientation is bisexual, which means they can be attracted to persons of either sex. (The "Kinsey scale," from Dr. Alfred Kinsey's famous 1948 report on human sexuality, suggests each person's orientation falls somewhere along a continuum, with exclusive heterosexuality at one end, exclusive homosexuality at the other end, and bisexuality in the middle.)

There is no respectable scientific data to suggest that, once set, sexual orientation is amenable to change. At a minimum, for the overwhelming majority of us, we simply are what we are. Sexual behavior can be altered, just as a left-handed person can be forced to write with his or her right hand. But in either instance, the person will be acting against his or her true nature. In the words of a late edition of the trusted Dr. Spock book on child rearing, "Experts agree that a person's basic or primary sexual orientation is set by the very earliest years of development."

The late Sylvia Pennington was a Pentecostal minister who set out to "save" gays by prayer and persuasion. But she ultimately concluded that they were instead damaged, maimed, scarred, and even killed by the well-meaning "ex-gay" ministries that purport to "cure" homosexuality. When one religion-oriented book was written about six gays who were supposedly "changed" to heterosexuals, Pennington noted, all six subjects soon provided the book's publisher with notarized statements that they had remained homosexual.

Dr. Keith Brodie, a former president of the American Psychiatric Association and later president of Duke University, agrees with Pennington. Mental health therapy to change sexual orientation, he says, "is about as successful as the handedness change, and about as painful, and also about as ludicrous."

And in 1994, the American Medical Association formally rejected the concept of "reparative" therapy designed to change sexual orientation. The organization acknowledged the obvious—that if gays experience emotional disturbance associated with their orientation, it probably stems from "a sense of alienation in an unaccepting environment." In other words, antigay social attitudes are bad for mental health.

Michael Bussee was a cofounder of Exodus International, perhaps the best known of the so-called "ex-gay" ministries. After five years with the group, he said he realized that the program not only had never changed a single person, but was actually doing a lot of harm. A forty-five-year-old Californian, Jack McIntyre, killed himself a year after signing up with an ex-gay ministry; he wrote in his suicide note that "no matter how much I prayed and tried to avoid temptation, I continually failed." Another disillusioned subject of such a ministry told a press conference that frustration had led him to mutilate his own genitals.

The central irony in these tragedies was captured by an observation made by a young lesbian I met shortly after she spent a year in one of the ex-gay programs in the Midwest. When we spoke, she was living with a Maryland PFLAG couple, recovering from the emotional scars left by the program. A formerly devout Catholic, she said she had thought about suicide while in the program—but that the worst part of the experience was that it threatened to destroy her own sense of spirituality. These so-called ministries, in short, tend to kill the very quality they purport to save.

Virtually every respected medical and mental health organization agrees that the ex-gay ministries can cause untold harm. A resolution of one of them, the American Psychiatric Association, lists the potential risks of "reparative therapy" as including depression, anxiety, and self-destructive behavior, in part because by definition the therapists' own antigay perspective just serves to reinforce the patient's central problem of self-hatred. Hence: "The APA opposes any psychiatric treatment . . . which is based on the prior assumption that homosexuality per se is a mental disorder or . . . the prior assumption that the patient should change his/her sexual orientation."

Most of us come to believe as youngsters that homosexuality is a heinous evil. And despite any subsequent overlays of intellectual sophistication, such early conditioning permanently shapes our perceptions. So it is hardly surprising that parents often make serious mistakes in dealing with their gay kids.

The stories of five such families make the point: Mary Griffith told her son he needed to pray harder to overcome his homosexual feelings. Cathy and Jonathan Tuerk subjected their eight-year-old son to psychotherapy to make him "more masculine." Marie Pridgen convinced her son to enter an ex-gay ministry to change his orientation. Sue Brown took her daughter to two psychiatrists to be "cured." Betty and Jim Holloran were estranged from their physician son for six years because they viewed him as a willful sinner.

Two of the children in these examples are dead. All of them suffered because of their parents' well-meaning mistakes. Ultimately, the parents all concluded that it was they and not their children whose behavior needed to change.

Mary Griffith's story perhaps reflects the ultimate human tragedy. She blames herself for the death of her son.

Mary says Bobby was "kind and gentle, with a fun-loving spirit." He was handsome, with clean-cut features and an Adonis-like body perfected by weight lifting. He loved old movies, particularly *The Seven Year Itch* with his favorite star, Marilyn Monroe. He loved Italian food and meeting people.

But the diary that he kept for the last two years of his life reveals a tortured soul. Tortured by passions he had been taught were sinful. Tortured by the bondage of what he called "society's rules." Tortured by fear of hell. "Gays are bad," he wrote, "and God sends bad people to Hell. . . . I guess I'm no good to anyone, not even God. Sometimes I feel like disappearing from the face of this earth."

The Griffiths attended Walnut Creek Presbyterian Church in Walnut Creek, California. There, Mary said, the ministers and the congregation were clear that homosexuals were sick, perverted, and condemned to eternal damnation. "And when they said that," Mary recalls, "I said, 'Amen.'"

For her part, Mary just knew that homosexuality was "an abomination to God." And even before she knew Bobby was gay, she conveyed her feelings to him in no uncertain terms. She remembers in sadness one incident that occurred when Bobby was fourteen. He had introduced her to a friend of his, a young girl. For some reason, Mary had loaned the girl a coat. Later, Mary learned that the girl had once had a lesbian encounter, and found herself unable to wear the coat again herself. "You can't love God and be gay," she told Bobby.

At about the same time, Bobby told his brother he was gay. Two years later, his brother told their parents. That night, the family was up until 4 A.M. talking and crying. They all agreed Bobby was a sinner, that he had to be cured by prayer and Christian counseling. Mary told him he had to repent or God would "damn him to hell and eternal punishment." She had faith that God would come to Bobby's rescue, but only if he read his Bible.

The Christian counselor recommended prayer and suggested that Bobby spend more time with his father. But Bobby's diary revealed that nothing was changing. "Why did you do this to me, God?" he wrote. "Am I going to hell? I need your seal of approval. If I had that, I would be happy. Life is so cruel and unfair."

His mother kept telling him he could change. "It seems like every time we talked, I would tell him that," she says. "I thought Bobby wasn't trying in his prayers." When Bobby became more withdrawn, she simply chalked it up to God's punishment. "Now," she says, "I look back and realize he was just depressed."

When Bobby was twenty, in desperation the Griffiths decided he should move to Portland, Oregon, and live with a cousin. At first, the move seemed to help. He worked as a nurse's aide in a senior citizens' home and developed something of a social life. But the depression returned and deepened. A few months later, in his diary, he cursed God and added, "I'm completely worthless as far as I'm concerned. What do you say to that? I don't care." Again and again, he emphasized the shame and self-blame he felt over his sexual orientation. "I am evil and wicked. I am dirt," he wrote. "My voice is small and unheard, unnoticed, damned."

One Friday night in August 1983, Bobby had dinner with his cousin. She noticed that he seemed thoughtful, perhaps depressed. He seemed to want to talk about something, but said little. Then he left, saying he was taking a bus to go dancing downtown.

Early the next morning, two men driving to work noticed a young man, later identified as Bobby, on an overpass above a busy thoroughfare. As they described the next few moments, the boy walked to the railing, turned around, and did a sudden back flip into mid-air. He landed in the path of an eighteen-wheeler.

Bobby's body was returned to Walnut Creek for funeral services in the Presbyterian church. The minister told the mourners that Bobby was gay, and suggested that his tragic end was the result of his sinning.

Later, the Griffiths met with their pastor for grief counseling. In her despair, Mary was seeking ways to atone for the loss of Bobby. She told the pastor she knew there were "other Bobbys out there" and asked how she could help them. The pastor merely shrugged his shoulders—and Mary never again returned to that church.

However, she did not lose her sense of religion. Her speech resonates with the tones of spiritual awareness. But she has found a very different God from the one she worshiped at Walnut Creek Presbyterian. She reread her Bible with fresh eyes, and sought out secular books about homosexuality. She concluded that there was nothing wrong with Bobby, that "he was the kind of person God wanted him to be . . . an equal, lovable, valuable part of God's creation." She says now, "I helped instill false guilt in an innocent child's conscience."

Bobby Griffith's fate is not uncommon among gay youth. One

report chartered by the government suggests that gay adolescents are nearly three times more likely than other teens to attempt suicide. Some 30 percent of all youth suicides, it says, can be traced to the pressures generated by "a society that stigmatizes and discriminates against gays and lesbians."

But Bobby's story stands out for two reasons. Unlike other youths who kill themselves, Bobby left an extensive written record of his anguish. And unlike other parents, his mother has not denied or buried her role in the tragedy, but has leveraged her remorse into aid to others.

Shortly after Bobby's death, Mary Griffith discovered PFLAG. For some years, she was president of an East San Francisco Bay PFLAG chapter and appeared frequently on television talk shows, usually wearing a button with Bobby's picture and another with the PFLAG message, "We love our gay and lesbian children." She has cooperated in the filming of documentaries about the Griffith family tragedy, and is the subject of the book *Prayers for Bobby: A Mother's Coming to Terms with the Suicide of Her Gay Son*, by Leroy Aarons, founder of the National Lesbian and Gay Journalists Association and a former national correspondent for the *Washington Post*. She campaigns tirelessly for the cause of public-school counseling supportive of gay teenagers, believing that Bobby would still be alive if his high school had had such a program.

And she has a guiding standard for other parents. Listen to your instincts as a mother or father, she tells them, not to those who urge you to violate your parental conscience. "All we had to do was say, 'We love you, Bobby, and we accept you,' and I know Bobby would be here today. Part of me wanted to reach out and tell him, 'You're fine just the way you are.' To me, that was my mother love, that was my conscience. But I didn't have the freedom to listen to my own conscience."

Like Mary Griffith, Catherine and Jonathan Tuerk were betrayed by the institution they respected above all others. For Griffith, it was her church. For the Tuerks, it was their profession

Catherine and Jonathan are both psychotherapists: she a nurse-practitioner with a private clientele, he a psychiatrist formerly with a world-famous hospital in Maryland. So when their little boy Joshua acted in what to them seemed inappropriate ways, they sent him to a psychiatrist—as often as four times a week, off and on, for nearly a decade. Ultimately, they spent tens of thousands of dollars in an endeavor that they now feel merely deepened Josh's insecurity and their own guilt.

The problem, as they saw it, was that Josh from infancy was more interested in "girl things" than in "boy things." In nursery school, he played with the girls in the dress-up room. On the playground, he shied away from the roughhousing of the other boys. When they gave him toy cars, instead of making them go "VROOM! VROOM!" he would play relationship games, calling one the "mommy car," another the "daddy car," When he played with the neighborhood children, he usually teamed with Tina, the girl next door, against the other boys. He spent a lot of time with Tina, because his interests seemed to mesh more with hers than with those of the other boys.

When Josh was six, his parents consulted a well-known child psychiatrist. In retrospect, the prescription they were given might as well have come from an anthology of old wives' tales: Josh should play contact sports and do more things with his father.

So they tried him at football, lacrosse, baseball, and basketball. Jonathan even took a turn at coaching Josh's soccer team. But nothing worked. Josh tried hard to carry out his parents' wishes, but he remained frightened and miserable. His only—partial—success came in karate, which in general he hated: he won a prize for form.

Meanwhile, when he was eight, his parents started sending him to psychotherapy to build his self-esteem and thereby, they hoped, help him grow up to be more masculine. Although he usually came home from these sessions looking sad, his parents were convinced that the short-term pain would produce long-term gain. Ultimately, Cathy thought, "he wouldn't be gay, and then he could be happy."

But at age nine, Josh wrote in his diary, "I hate myself. I think I'm a fag." And twelve years later, he told his parents the words they had for so long been dreading: he was gay. (When one of his former neighborhood playmates learned of that, his surprised response was, "How can that be? He always had that thing going with Tina.")

The Tuerks finally decided they had been tilting at windmills. Ultimately, Jonathan resigned from the American Psychoanalytic Association—dissatisfied, among other things, with the analytic profession's slowness to acknowledge the degree to which sexual orientation might be innate and unchangeable.

Cathy's experience has led her to work with researchers at Johns Hopkins University who study what she calls "gentle" boys—those (like Kevyn Aucoin, see Chapter 5) who shun more macho pursuits in favor of the intellectual or artistic. Some such youngsters turn out to be heterosexual, just as a number of competitive, athletic types turn out to be gay. Cathy tries to show parents that they can accept their children for whatever they are. Recent studies have led to increasing recognition of a so-called "sissy-boy" syndrome that does appear to be a relatively reliable indicator of homosexuality. Boys fitting the syndrome often, for example, enjoy playing with dolls; their behavior even at age four and five can be quite effeminate. Usually, such behavior tends to become far less noticeable after age eight, probably reflecting a surrender to social norms.

To Cathy, the implications for parents are clear. Fighting the inevitable is more than a waste of time. It can boomerang in cruel fashion. As she now sees it: "At the age of twenty-one, Josh decided to be himself. My son was born gay. I know it."

Marie Pridgen of Wilmington, North Carolina, says that when her son Crae told her he was gay, "I was a crazy parent stuck up there on the ceiling for a while. . . . I even went to the bars, and pulled him out and preached to his friends in the bars. I did things a crazy parent does."

At one point, when he was considering marrying a girlfriend, Crae consulted his minister about his attraction to men. The minister and he prayed together. When they were done, the minister told Crae, "Go home. You're healed." But his feelings remained unchanged, and Crae wisely refrained from marrying.

Marie prevailed upon Crae to enroll in an ex-gay ministry in California in an effort to change his orientation. But after about six months, they both decided the venture was not only worthless but potentially harmful.

Marie, devoutly religious, attended a Presbyterian church in Wilmington. She turned to the church for help, and there, fortunately, found relief from her anguish. For one thing, her minister was sympathetic to gay concerns; he even delivered a sermon on homosexuality explaining that gays, like everyone else, are simply looking for love and acceptance.

The church also housed a support group for parents of gay children. It stressed the importance of unconditional love to their children, and helped Marie change her ways. "I thought, 'Hey, that's my child and I love him.' I hadn't been helping him. I was just destroying a relationship."

Then, when Crae was twenty-nine, he was beaten and severely injured by three Marines who were angry over then President Clinton's proposals to liberalize military policy toward gay service members. According to news reports, as the Marines were pummeling Crae they shouted, "Clinton must pay, all you faggots are going to die." A police officer told the *New York Times* that the Marines later showed no remorse and said they hated all homosexuals and were "not ashamed of it."

The incident became the focus of high-level meetings in the White House and at the Pentagon, and Crae and Marie were flown to Washington to sit in. On Capitol Hill, they visited the offices of several senators who expressed outrage over the incident. In a Capitol corridor, they were recognized by then First Lady, now Senator, Hillary Clinton, who approached them to express her own sympathies.

In the next few days, Marie and Crae made a series of media appearances together, including *The Today Show*, *Dateline*, and other talk shows. The *Dateline* broadcast ended with a close-up of Marie, tense with emotion, responding to a question on whether the events had made her afraid: "I'm not only afraid for my own life and my son's life," she said, "but for every American who stands up for what's right."

When her daughter Cody was fifteen, Sue Brown chanced to overhear a romantic conversation between Cody and another girl. Sue confronted Cody, who confirmed that she was gay. Groping for consolation, Sue compared homosexuality to the dangers of drug addiction. "At least this isn't going to kill you," she said to Cody. Her daughter replied, "Mother, I've already tried to kill myself."

So Sue took her to a psychiatrist. "She said there was nothing wrong with my daughter, that I had homophobia," Sue recalls. They consulted a psychotherapist, who said essentially the same thing.

Mother and daughter conspired to keep the news from Cody's father; meanwhile, Sue found PFLAG and attended meetings regularly. After a few years of this secrecy, Sue one day called Cody, who was by then in college: it was time to come out to her father. Sue was planning to march with PFLAG in the gay-pride parade that weekend, and it was possible her husband might see her. Cody rushed home to break the news to her father, but he was not as accepting as Sue. Their differing reactions to Cody's gayness became one of the issues that led to their ultimate divorce.

Somewhat later, Sue was interviewed by Barbara Bartucci for a *Woman's Day* article about PFLAG. During one telephone call, Bartucci heard what she called "tinkly party sounds" on Sue's end. Sue explained that she was holding a reception following a Methodist ceremony of union for Cody and Julie Marria. At one point, Sue excused herself to talk with someone. When she returned to the call, she said that the voice in the background was that of "my daughter-in-law, Julie."

In her article, Bartucci wrote: "Her daughter-in-law, I thought. She means her daughter's female partner. The naturalness of the phrase—the loving acceptance those words implied—touched me." The author described the incident as one that "defines a healthy relationship between a parent and a homosexual child."

Sue moved a long way from the mother who had once taken her child to a psychiatrist. Among other things, she turned her house into a haven for gay teenagers whose parents had ejected them from their own homes; they would stay with Sue until their parents, in her words, "become educated," or until the youngsters finished high school and could live on their own.

The *Washington Post Magazine* cover story was headed, "The Bittersweet Life of Jimmy Holloran." It began this way:

> *He had it all—looks, brains, startling athletic ability. Then he had a falling out with his parents and his church over his homosexuality, and left for a new life in San Francisco. After he got AIDS 14 years later, he did the only thing a beloved son could do. He came home to die.*

Jimmy was an honor student and president of the student council in his Washington, D.C., high school, and is in the school's athletic hall of fame as a running back on the school's city championship team. He won a national high school poetry contest, and thought he might become a priest. He turned down a scholarship to Harvard in order to attend Holy Cross, a Catholic college.

At Holy Cross, he was all–New England on a baseball team that twice played in the College World Series. As a senior, he scored higher than anyone before him on the Harvard medical school entrance exam. After graduating from medical school and serving his internship, he became head of an emergency room at a hospital in San Francisco. There, he also produced film documentaries, including an award-winning medical film about AIDS.

One evening, Jimmy telephoned his parents, Jim and Betty, from San Francisco to tell them he was gay. He asked them to accept him as a gay man. But no matter how much they loved him, they just couldn't do that.

They were ashamed of him. Their Catholicism told them he was a sinner. To Jim and Betty, Jimmy had tossed away his faith and was acting reprehensibly. Every time they went to church, they prayed for his salvation. Jimmy was offended by their attitude, and virtually stopped talking to them.

Six unhappy years passed in this fashion; then Jimmy learned he had AIDS. He didn't tell his parents until he was seriously ill and hospitalized in San Francisco. In the face of this crisis, questions of faith faded in importance, and Jim and Betty went to San Francisco. Their attitude toward homosexuality began to thaw in the aura of warmth and caring they found emanating from his friends there. When they returned to Washington, they sought out help and found PFLAG. Increasingly, they found themselves questioning the plausibility of their church's stance on homosexuality, and in Jimmy's final illness, they attained a more meaningful closeness with him. Jimmy spent his last months in the family home, surrounded by his parents, his three brothers, and his sister. Jim and Betty regretted the years they had missed being with him because they hadn't accepted him as he was. But they now offered prayers of thanks for the time they still had together.

In the face of harsh religious objections from relatives and friends, Betty became a champion of Catholics with AIDS and their families. After Jimmy's death, she volunteered at an AIDS hospice and collected clothing and furniture for those living there. She worked with the families of people with AIDS and conducted workshops on coming out to parents, for people with HIV and AIDS, at both a national PFLAG convention and an International Gay and Lesbian Health Conference.

During virtually the entire time of her service to families touched by AIDS, Betty herself was terminally ill. Five years after Jimmy's death, she herself died of cancer.

Perhaps the most courageous thing she and Jim did was going public with the family's tale via that *Washington Post Magazine* cover story. It triggered animosity within their church and among their own relatives. But it also brought warm responses of gratitude, evidenced by a thick file of thank-you letters and accolades from priests and parishioners.

Veronica and Jerry Colfer (see chapter 2) were among the Catholics inspired by Betty Holloran's work. Vocal and articulate critics of their church's antigay stance, the Colfers attracted considerable media attention, and Betty would probably endorse one of Veronica's oft-quoted observations: "Families were here before churches."

4

The Birth of a Movement

Jeanne Manford is a slender, mild-mannered elementary school teacher who in 1972, armed only with a homemade sign, touched off a revolution among parents of gay children. Writing decades later in the *New York Times*, Pulitzer Prize winner and novelist Anna Quindlen would describe PFLAG's pioneer mother as a woman who made history by standing by her son and writing "her unconditional love on poster paper for all the world to see."

It was a time when police were still raiding gay bars and arresting the patrons. Homosexuality was formally classified as a mental illness. Physical attacks on gays were a matter of total indifference to police. Gays were subject to arrest simply for being gay.

Jeanne cannot explain why, in such a hostile climate, she was not upset when she and her husband, Jules, learned their son Morty was gay. She wasn't so naive that she didn't recognize the stigma attached to being gay. But she loved Morty, and she told him that whatever made him happy was fine with her.

Jeanne was then in her fourth year at P.S. 32, a half-block away from the Manfords' Flushing, New York home. She would ultimately spend twenty-six peaceful years teaching the neighborhood youngsters. But her calm, competent schoolroom manner masked a fiercely protective parental instinct that surfaced in her personal life.

In the early 1970s, Morty was a student at Columbia University. He was also a pioneer gay-rights activist, having founded one of the first gay campus organizations. (He later was an early president of one of the original gay-rights groups, the Gay Activists Alliance.) So as perhaps was inevitable, Jeanne got a call from the police one night at 1 A.M. Morty had been arrested. "And you know," the officer added ominously, "he's homosexual."

Jeanne was stung to anger. "I know that. Why are you bothering him? Why don't you go after criminals and stop harassing gays?"

Morty, standing near the police officer, didn't hear what his mother had said. But he saw the officer scratching his head in astonishment after he put down the phone.

The incident that would give rise to the family movement now known as PFLAG occurred in early 1972. While handing out leaflets at a political gathering in New York City, Morty was attacked by the president of the New York City firemen's union, a former Golden Gloves champion. Police officers stood and watched as the man beat Morty and pushed him down a stairwell. Morty was hospitalized and had to take painkillers for a week.

Jeanne was furious. What right did they have to assault her son? Why didn't the police protect him? What kind of police force did New York have? Her lifelong restraint dissolved in anger. Nobody could walk over Morty like that!

She telephoned the *New York Times*, but they kept hanging up on her. So she fired off a letter to the *New York Post* expressing her outrage, particularly at the police for doing nothing. It was printed, and suddenly she was a celebrity of sorts. New Yorkers were amazed that a mother would speak out on behalf of her gay son. Among the most amazed were Morty's friends, who found it hard to believe his mother would actually say publicly, "I have a homosexual son, and I love him."

As a result of her letter, the entire family found itself in demand by television talk shows. Jeanne, Jules, and Morty appeared together in Boston and Cincinnati, and Jeanne and Jules did other shows in New Orleans, Detroit, and Toronto. These were the first of more than fifty television appearances that Jeanne would make, including on major shows such as *Donahue*.

The publicity drew waves of response from parents of gay children, and the Manfords began to sense the need for a parents' organization. The final impetus in that direction came in June 1972, when Morty asked his parents to march with him in a gay-pride parade.

For Morty, the parade was a very special event, for he had been present at the incident that gave rise to the very concept of gay pride. This was the Stonewall Rebellion, and it represented a sort of gay Declaration of Independence. It occurred on June 28, 1969, when police raided the Stonewall Inn, a gay bar on Christopher Street in Greenwich Village. Unlike in earlier raids, the patrons decided they had had enough of police injustice. About two hundred of them resisted arrest, taunted the police, and threw bottles, rocks, and even their shoes at the officers. The next night, more demonstrations flared up, and the protests continued for five days. In other cities, rallies were held to support the New York uprising and to protest similar treatment of gays around the country. Stonewall became a symbol of rebellion and defiant self-respect that spread to gay communities throughout the nation.

Gay-pride celebrations, held in commemoration of the Stonewall uprising, are now commonplace even in smaller cities. But to Morty—who had been in the Stonewall Inn when the police arrived—the second annual New York parade in 1972 still had immediate and intimate significance. Jeanne agreed to go with him, but only if Morty would help her make a sign she could carry. She had to let people know why she was marching. So they hand-lettered a cardboard sign: "Parents of Gays: Unite in Support for Our Children."

Jules couldn't attend the parade, and Jeanne carried the sign alone, walking next to Morty. The ovation was overwhelming. For the first few blocks, Jeanne assumed the wild cheering, shouting, and applause were for Dr. Benjamin Spock, the famed baby doctor, who was marching just behind her. But then young people began running up to her, crying, screaming, hugging her, kissing her, asking her if she would talk to their parents.

The idea of a parents' group took shape in her mind. As they marched, she and Morty discussed the possibility. At home, the Manfords' telephone rang constantly for days. It was clear that parents needed a place where they could talk to each other and know they were not alone. A place where they could hear others say there was nothing wrong with their kids.

Morty helped publicize the first meeting. He and a friend, writer Barbara Love, placed an ad in the *Village Voice*. They called other friends. They posted notices in bookstores and bars.

The first formal meeting was held in March 1973 in the Metropolitan Duane Methodist Church in Greenwich Village, by invitation of a sympathetic minister, Reverend Ed Egan. About twenty people—half of them parents, half of them young gays—were on hand for the historic occasion.

Meetings were held monthly there for the next twenty years, until they were moved in 1992 to Community Church in midtown Manhattan.

The next major step in the movement came in the summer of 1974, when Jeanne and Jules, visiting in Los Angeles, met Adele and Larry Starr, who had a gay son. The two couples had dinner together, and the Manfords' exciting conversation about their experiences prompted Adele to try to start a Los Angeles group.

It was at first a frustrating task. "We called a meeting in 1975, but nobody came," Adele remembers ruefully. But she tried again in March 1976, and this time thirty-five people showed up. A West Coast counterpart of the Manfords' group was underway.

Meanwhile, other small support groups had been forming independently around the country. Betty Fairchild, the author of a still-popular 1976 book, *Now That You Know*, personally founded two groups, one in Washington, D.C., in 1974 and another in Denver two years later. A St. Louis group was started by Marion and Art Wirth and Carolyn Griffin, authors of another popular book for parents, *Beyond Acceptance*. Others were beginning in cities such as Phoenix, Boston, Seattle, Anchorage, Pensacola, Baltimore, Kansas City (Missouri), Houston, and San Francisco. Gradually, members of the scattered groups found each other, often as the result of radio and television appearances by some of the more "out" parents, such as the Manfords and Starrs. A word-of-mouth network grew.

The first national meeting took place in Washington, D.C., in 1979, organized largely by Fairchild and a member of her group to coincide with that year's first-ever national march for gay rights. One highlight of the weekend was the appearance of two parents—Adele Starr and Dick Ashworth, a New York lawyer who had become a mainstay of the Manfords' group—addressing a major Mall rally.

As the crowds roared, Ashworth and Starr called for equal protection under the law for their gay children. Said Ashworth: "It is time for the world to realize that we parents of gays will support our children and fight for their rights." Said Starr: "They, and we, will not settle for less than their full rights in pursuit of happiness."

The following day, parents from around the country met in the First Congregational Church in Washington to talk about forming a national organization. It didn't happen right then, but a foundation was laid and the various groups kept in closer touch. Two years later, in the summer of 1981, PFLAG was officially founded.

The organizing took place during a weekend meeting at the Starrs' Los Angeles home. Thirty-one representatives came from a variety of cities and towns—from New York City to Rifle, Colorado (population about 4,000). The location and timing arose from the fact that Dick and Amy Ashworth, who had two gay sons, were in California for the wedding of their third and only non-gay son.

In a marathon two-day session punctuated by frequent pizza deliveries, the founders chose the organization's name and logo, adopted a statement of purpose, elected a board of directors, and assigned Dick Ashworth the task of incorporation. Adele Starr became PFLAG's first president and Dick Ashworth the first chair of its board.

By the next summer, the organization was strong enough to hold its first national convention, in Los Angeles. It was both a proud and sad Jeanne Manford who attended. Her vision of a national organization of parents seeking justice for their gay children had come to pass. But that very first convention was dedicated to her husband, Jules, who had died earlier in 1982.

For the next several years, PFLAG's national headquarters was

Adele Starr's den, which served as an information clearinghouse and record storehouse. Slowly, new support groups started up throughout the country, in small towns as well as large cities. It wasn't always easy for the pioneering parents. In semirural Iowa, for example, a mother who had been president of her local church congregation was deposed and ostracized after forming a parents' group that, at first, met in her church. But in ten years the original handful of groups grew to nearly 250, and the larger chapter meetings, as in Denver, sometimes drew one hundred people or more. In 1989, a genuine national office was opened in Washington, D.C. And in 1990, Tom Sauerman of Philadelphia, a Lutheran pastor with a gay son, became the first executive director.

A decade of growth was celebrated at PFLAG's tenth annual convention in Charlotte, North Carolina, in 1991. There, "The Los Angeles 31" were honored by more than five hundred people at the Omni Charlotte Hotel. Among the emotion-choked speakers were Adele Starr and Amy Ashworth. Adele said the founders had been praised for their courage, but that courage was not involved: "We did it out of love and anger and a sense of injustice, and because we had to tell the world the truth about our children." Amy said she was embarrassed by the tribute, "because what we did is something that comes naturally—we love our children."

Once again, though, for Jeanne Manford, a milestone PFLAG convention was an occasion of sadness. Morty was ill with AIDS, and she missed the meeting. Morty had once proclaimed, "The family that marches together, stays together," but death took him from the family in 1992.

"I will always love my son. I always thought he was extra-special,"

Jeanne says. Nor did his death quell her dedication to combating antigay prejudice. The spunk that moved her to carry that sign in 1972 was apparent twenty years later, just weeks after Morty's death, when she faced down a notorious gay-baiter on a raucous episode of the television show *Geraldo*.

The show featured two young same-sex couples, each of whom had recently attended their high school proms. But attention was soon focused on two invited audience guests, Jeanne and a discredited psychologist named Paul Cameron.

Cameron had long been known in the media as an especially vicious apologist for homophobia. For many years, his condescending tone and tight-lipped smile of superiority had been a frequent feature of sensationalist TV and radio talk shows.

On *Geraldo*, over and again, he needled Jeanne for having loved and supported her son. His persistent hostility ultimately enraged not only most of the studio audience but even Rivera himself. At one point, Cameron referred to Jeanne as a "poor woman" for having had a gay son. The remark brought her leaping to her feet, and she told Cameron heatedly, "I'm not a poor woman. . . . I can certainly hold my head up higher than anyone who has been thrown out of his professional association!" Her words were practically drowned in cheers. (It turned out that Cameron had in fact many years before, in 1983, been stripped of his membership in the American Psychological Association.)

In 1993, Jeanne organized yet another PFLAG group, which met in her home until it grew too large and moved to a nearby church. In June of that year, as grand marshal of the first gay pride celebration held in her borough of Queens, New York, she basked in a five-minute ovation of gratitude from a cheering, whistling, stomping crowd.

THE BIRTH OF A MOVEMENT

In her *New York Times* piece, Anna Quindlen wrote of Jeanne:

> *She loved and accepted her child the way he was. In a perfect*
> *world, this would be the definition of "parent" in the dictionary.*
> *The point is not what you'll tell your friends at the bridge table.*
> *It is what you'll tell yourself in the end.*

Perhaps someday Jeanne Manford's accepting response will be typical of parents who learn they have a gay child. Perhaps a child's gayness will be no more unsettling than if he or she were left-handed. And perhaps no one will dream of defining a class of people by their sexual identity any more than by their eye color or taste in literature.

Don't hold your breath.

Pending that utopian day, gayness remains near the top of most Americans' lists of social stigmata. Thus, an organization like PFLAG remains acutely needed. For too many parents, the point is indeed what they'll tell their friends at the bridge table.

Some become literally sick about what others might think. Harriet Dart, for example, became critically ill with asthma. Her doctor suggested she walk up to the first person she met after leaving his office and say, "Guess what? I have a gay son." He told her, "If they have an asthma attack, that's their problem. But if you have another one it will kill you."

So Harriet sought out the PFLAG group in Rochester, New York, where she was then living. For a time, as for so many others, the organization became for her a sort of emergency first-aid station. (Later, when she and her husband, Bill, moved to Detroit, they founded a PFLAG chapter there, and Harriet became head of chapter development for the national organization.)

This type of rescue operation is one arm of PFLAG's three-part mission: support, education, and advocacy. For "new" parents, the need for support is usually paramount. The peer group meetings—attended largely by parents, with a sprinkling of young gays—often provide the first opportunity for traumatized parents to vent their often intense distress.

For most of life's crises, it's easy to find others who will support you. Death, illness, accident, and job loss are common occurrences for which others are quick to come to your side, to listen and understand and soothe. When you're hurting, you don't want to have to convince others of your pain—you want instant empathy. But after learning you have a gay child, it may seem that there is nowhere you can turn for solace. So a PFLAG support meeting often provides the first safe haven for the relief of pent-up emotions. There, you can find that instant empathy. You don't have to pretend you're not feeling anger, grief, shame, guilt.

"It's just an incredible experience when you finally realize you're not alone," says Cathy Tuerk of Washington, D.C. "There's a kind of unconditional acceptance. You see others who have survived and are at different stages of the process of acceptance. It's encouraging to hear them remember how they felt when they first knew."

Those who have "survived" become role models. "We get to help others," says a father. "It gives us a sense of our own progress and strength. It's really empowering."

Education, the second arm of PFLAG's mission, is an important aspect of the support process itself. Parents and other kin ultimately move to acceptance, and beyond, largely because of what they learn—and unlearn—about homosexuality.

PFLAG's education function reaches far beyond the support groups and into the mainstream. To this end, it utilizes publications, fact sheets, reading lists, cassettes, conferences, seminars, and speaker bureaus. The most effective teaching agents, however, are PFLAG members themselves. Newly educated, legions of parents are moved to pass on what they've learned to their schools, churches, community organizations, and government officials.

Advocacy, the final facet of PFLAG's mission, clearly overlaps with education. In a sense, advocacy is simply education applied to points of political leverage—voting blocs or public bodies—to attain particular ends, such as equal-rights measures or broader sex education. For PFLAG members, called PFLAGgers, are convinced that when Americans learn the truth about homosexuality, their sense of fairness will not allow them to continue to discriminate against our gay kids.

When that happens, PFLAG's mission will have been fulfilled. Education and advocacy will have generated the ultimate instrument of family support: a society in which parents will have no reason to lament having a gay child. It will be a society in which Jeanne Manford's nonchalance about her son's coming out will be the parental norm.

And PFLAG will no longer have any reason to exist.

5

Growing Up Gay

Some young people literally would rather die than let their parents or the world know they are gay.

Leonard Jenkins was fourteen when he was saved by another student who found him hanging by his neck from a rafter in an Akron high school storage building. After the incident, the school counselor told Leonard's mother, Rada, that he would "rather his kid came home with cancer" than be gay.

If you are a parent upset by the disclosure that your child is gay, your discomfort almost certainly pales by comparison to what he or she has already experienced. And you should take comfort in the fact that— by the very act of coming out to you—your child has shown exemplary honesty, trust and courage. To grow up gay is to feel that much of society considers you repugnant—sick, sinful or worse. "It's a burden that few of us could bear without severe emotional damage," says Father Robert Nugent, a priest who has ministered to gay Catholics.

Statistics as to the number of teen suicides owing to sexual orientation are obviously hard to come by, since the kind of shame that produces the deadly despair virtually ensures secrecy about its cause. But researchers' estimates of the proportion of teen suicides due to same-sex orientation have run as high as thirty percent. Whatever the number, many others self-destruct more indirectly, through the avenues of substance abuse or promiscuity.

In many ways, the cultural climate has improved significantly for teenage gays since the 1980s, when my daughter Bobbi was in school. Across society, we are at least more aware, if not yet genuinely accepting, of the commonness of homosexuality. Movies and television now regularly portray gay characters, often sympathetically. Openly gay role models are increasingly visible in virtually all levels of society. One result is that gay youth are coming out at earlier ages; my guess is that under today's conditions, Bobbi would have come out, certainly to herself and probably to us, years earlier than she did.

Still, the path to adulthood for any gay child remains strewn with cultural land mines. For many, the threat of parental rejection—even of finding themselves homeless, physically evicted from the family home—is as real as ever. And for virtually all, their schools continue to nurture a virulent homophobia that can turn every school day into one of dread.

If it seems shocking that a school official would tell Rada Jenkins he'd rather his child have cancer than be gay, that counselor is hardly a schoolhouse oddity. Administrative indifference or hostility remains a potent threat to the well-being of millions of youth.

Ask James Nabozny. In Ashland, Wisconsin, schoolmates taunted, bullied, beat, mock-raped, and urinated on him; they pelted him with steel nuts and bolts and kicked him in the stomach until he bled internally. He and his parents begged school officials for protection, but say they failed even to get any sympathy. A principal told James that "boys will be boys," and that because he was openly gay, he should "expect" such treatment from other students.

Or ask Derek Henkle. In Reno, Nevada, tormentors also pelted him with metal objects, lassoed him around the neck, threatened to drag him behind a truck, and ultimately drove him to an emotional breakdown. When he complained, a principal on one occasion told him to "stop acting like a fag" and a vice principal in another instance just laughed.

James and Derek both sued their schools and received handsome out-of-court settlements. So the steep price paid by the Ashland and Reno school systems perhaps will serve to warn administrators around the country that they need to start paying attention to the well-being of all their students.

Hopeful signs are on the horizon. An Illinois high school recently voted a lesbian pair its "cutest couple." Same-sex female and male couples occasionally are welcomed, or at least tolerated, at high school proms. And in some 1,200 schools, organizations known as Gay-Straight Alliances (GSAs) now exist, if often on perilously shaky foundations. The GSA experiences—one dramatic story is described in some detail later in this chapter—demonstrate both the progress and frustrations inherent in the process of uprooting deep prejudices.

The time of decent treatment for all students alike will, someday, arrive. But don't hold your breath. These pioneering probes into encrusted barriers of hatred and fear, however welcome, remain relatively few, tentative, and fragile. If 1,200 schools have GSAs, tens of thousands do not. In most, students are far too fearful—reasonably so, for the most part—to attempt to form support groups. And in others, they are prevented by school officials from doing so.

In Salt Lake City, before finally relenting four years later, administrators banned all extracurricular clubs rather than allow a GSA. In Boyd County, Kentucky, officials likewise banned all groups—although the superintendent of schools admitted to the *New York Times* that he was trying to maintain the traditional clubs by sneaking them into the classroom curriculum. (One Bible group met in the hallway before school.) The would-be GSA sponsor, English teacher and certified counselor Kaye King, said she was ordered to not even say hello to one student whose parents feared he could be "turned" gay.

Many school officials simply ignore the law—the Equal Access Act, signed by President Reagan in 1984—that requires them to treat all extracurricular groups alike. In Klein, Texas, an upscale suburb of Houston, administrators concocted a series of rules, changes, and delays that prevented Marla Dukler, a sixteen-year-old lesbian junior, from forming a GSA. And the principal even forbade the school newspaper from writing about the disagreement within the student body—which saw Marla called "faggot" and "dyke" and body-slammed into a wall of lockers, even while other students were signing a petition supporting her plan. Only after Marla brought suit did the district relent and allow her to form the GSA.

Members of other minority groups can look to their own families for understanding, support, guidance, and role models. "You're a fine human being," the old black man tells his granddaughter on the television series *I'll Fly Away.* "You're as good as anyone else and don't you ever let anyone tell you different." But gay kids typically are terrified, often with good cause, of parental rejection; so even those parents who might be supportive are not told. John Favretto, who grew up gay in Bethesda, Maryland, puts it succinctly: "We can't come home crying and say, 'The straight kids made fun of me at school today.'"

Inevitably, much of the energy of gay teens typically goes into maintaining a web of deception about their sexual orientation. They perceive, correctly, that candor could bring not only rejection by family and friends, but also physical jeopardy. The psychological toll is daunting. By staying mute for some years, says Amanda Schlesinger of St. Paul, Minnesota, she saved herself a certain amount of grief from others, but left "a black spot of shame and pain deep inside me." She says, "Every time I stayed quiet, I was killing myself from the inside out."

At a minimum, coming out publicly is an act of high courage. It is, among other things, a decision to be on guard for the rest of your life.

Perhaps the premier instance of antigay savagery is the highly publicized murder of twenty-one-year-old Matthew Shepherd, a slight, gentle, openly gay college student in Laramie, Wyoming. Tied by two thugs to a fence outside town and left hanging crucifix-style in near-freezing temperature, Matt was discovered eighteen hours later by two motorcyclists who at first thought the body was a scarecrow. Hospitalized, comatose for five days, he died on October 12, 1998. At his funeral, reporters counted sixteen antigay protesters, religious extremists, marching outside.

For many, tragically, the danger comes from their own families.

The New York Times told of a gay boy whose arm was deeply lacerated because his father had thrown him through a glass door; it told of another whose face was badly scarred because his mother had burned him so he "would not be attractive to other men." The father of another boy named Matthew, a National Honor Society high schooler in Illinois, screamed, "I brought you into this world, I can take you out," and choked him until he passed out; when Matthew came to, he packed his belongings and left, never to see his parents again. Bryan Chinn, a Huntington,

West Virginia tenth grader, lived with his grandmother but says when she learned he was gay, she "threw my clothes out the window."

To Lyn, who grew up in Southern California, expulsion from her family home might have been preferable to what did happen. She says her mother had her locked up in a mental hospital. There, she says, she was subjected to "aversion therapy" consisting of, among other horrors, being given medication to nauseate her and then being shown pornographic pictures of girls. As a crowning irony, her mother sent her a get-well card!

Gay teenagers evicted by their parents turn up daily on the doorstep of New York City's Hetrick-Martin Institute, which provides social services, education, and advocacy for gay and lesbian adolescents. More than a quarter of all gay and lesbian youth who come out to their parents are actually thrown out of their homes, according to one Institute estimate.

But whatever their home situation, the archvillain for gay kids remains the schoolhouse culture. To the average teen, peer pressure typically is all-powerful. High school "social hierarchies take the power away from the parents" and become the "dominant authority," says Christopher Rice, gay son of best-selling novelist Anne Rice and now a novelist in his own right (see Chapter 10).

So it is, often tragically, that the influence of insensitive schools, complicated by religious pressures, can at least temporarily outweigh that of even the most loving of parents. Consider what happened to Michael Larson.

Michael knew from age nine that he was gay but feared to tell anyone, particularly his devoutly religious parents, Bonnie and John. But when he was twenty, suicidal thoughts led him to confide in an Episcopal priest, and the priest recommended an organization called Regeneration, which promised to help him "change" his orientation. That didn't work, and Michael was wracked by shame over what he felt was a terrible character flaw. He sought solace in furtive sex and was arrested in a police stakeout of a public park. In desperation, he turned to his last hope. He called home and confessed all to his parents.

To Michael's surprise, they told him that while they didn't understand, they loved and accepted him; if he was gay, they would learn what they needed to know about that. Thus, it was at home that Michael found true regeneration. Within a few years, openly gay, he was in a committed relationship and running his own business in Charlotte, North Carolina.

Why are parents generally so ill-equipped to handle the news? A treasure of PFLAG tradition—a picture of the organization's founding mother, Jeanne Manford, marching beside her son Morty in New York's 1972 gay-pride parade—suggests part of the answer. In the foreground, Manford is carrying a hand-lettered sign saying, "Parents of Gays: Unite in Support for Our Children" (see Chapter 4). Marching behind her is Dr. Benjamin Spock, child-rearing guru to generations of American parents.

The irony of this tableau is pointed out by Robb Forman Dew, prize-winning novelist and active New Hampshire PFLAGer, in *The Family Heart*, her moving memoir about her son's coming out. She writes that her son first realized that he was "different" by the age of two or three, and notes that thirty percent of all teenage suicides result from the despair of gay and lesbian children. Nevertheless, she laments that neither Spock nor his fellow wizard of parenting, T. Berry Brazleton, had then offered any hint of a significant truth, namely, "that parents' assumptions of the heterosexuality of their sons or daughters begin at birth and are a threat to their children's lives."

Rare is the doctor or nurse who discusses this matter with young parents. Teachers, counselors, and sex educators, in theory, could help fill the void of ignorance for children as well as parents. Typically, however, conservative activists roll out the heavy cannons at the slightest threat of such enlightenment in public schools. Invoking "family values" and God, but often relying on archaic superstition and vicious rhetoric, they cow school boards and school officials into heeding their most preposterous statements. An example is a wild-eyed warning from the Dean of a state university in the Southwest: "Since the homosexuals cannot reproduce, they must out of necessity recruit . . . my children and grandchildren and yours." As a result, sex-education courses are outlawed or reduced to trivia. Potentially helpful books are banned or their access limited in school and in public libraries. Teachers and counselors, fearful for their positions, often dare not even speak in tolerant terms, much less show support for their frightened, besieged gay students.

The ignorance of many Americans and their apparent determination to stay that way were strikingly demonstrated by a national flap that arose over the comic strip "For Better or for Worse." Scores of newspapers across the country actually refused to run a four-week episode of the strip in which a teenager comes out to his best friend and his parents. A summary of the episode strikingly reveals the down-home warmth and common sense of which, thanks to censorship, hundreds of thousands of American newspaper readers were deprived.

The sequence involved an ordinary seventeen-year-old, Lawrence Poirier, who tells his friend Mike that he is gay. Mike initially has some difficulty with the news, but the boys' friendship prevails. However, when Lawrence tells his parents, they grow hysterical. Lawrence's mother demonstrates a series of common parental reactions:

- Disbelief: "I don't believe you." And, "It's a phase. You'll pass through it."
- Self-blame: "It's my fault. I was too protective. I should have pushed you harder." (To Lawrence's protestation that she is not to blame, she shouts, "I have to blame somebody!")
- Denial: "You are not gay! You are not."
- Finally, anger and desperation, as she calls for her husband: "Talk some sense into him!!!"

Lawrence's father instead kicks him out of the house, saying, "If that's the life you've chosen, I don't want you under this roof! . . . Go wherever 'your kind' hangs out!!!"

Later, repenting, the mother asks Mike to look for Lawrence and bring him home, where Lawrence is welcomed by his relieved parents. "I'm not going to judge you," his father says. "As long as you're a good man and a kind man I'll respect you. As for the rest, what will be will be, que sera sera." (The family later names their new puppy "Sera.") The warmth of the two boys' families ultimately triumphs over the initial shock of Lawrence's coming out.

The basic theme of the episode was that families can pull together and learn to accept even when they don't understand. But the rationale for censorship offered by the editor of one newspaper reveals much of society's thoughtless misunderstanding on the subject. His newspaper, the editor wrote, was merely drawing the line "between live-and-let-live tolerance and love-me-love-my-lifestyle advocacy." Thus, he said, the decision merely supported Americans' general refusal "to grant full social approval to homosexual lifestyles."

The strip had said nothing about lifestyles of any kind. It gave no indication that Lawrence even had a boyfriend, much less that he had had homosexual relations. Rather, it simply dealt with an inner experience—the hormonal reality that he was attracted to men rather than to women. And what the strip did say—for example, that the parents did not rule out the possibility that their son could be both gay and "a good man and a kind man"—had nothing to do with advocacy of any sort. It might well, however, have saved the lives of some despairing young readers.

This uproar over a comic strip demonstrates how gay people have been demonized—conceived as weird, alien creatures who are wholly different from the rest of us plain folk. Thus, an editor can look at an episode portraying a young man's emotions and see it as endorsing some sort of subversive lifestyle. An otherwise loving father, as in the strip itself, can order his son to go "wherever 'your kind' hangs out." The immense cruelty of these attitudes is reflected in the son's poignant response, as he cries out in the darkness outside the house, "What do you mean 'my kind.' My name is Lawrence Poirier—and I live here!!!"

While our homophobic culture drives some gay kids to self-destruct, legions of them obviously survive, stronger for having overcome the obstacles. And if most heterosexual teenagers remain hostile to their gay schoolmates, there is encouraging evidence that some straight kids are beginning to rally around the cause of those who are not.

Kevyn Aucoin is an example of one for whom the difficulties of growing up gay seem to have forged strength of character.

And the experience of Jennifer Peters is a heart warming sign that, albeit slowly and painfully, times and attitudes will change in our schools.

Kevyn's story, however instructive, is in many ways far from typical. Of keenly artistic bent, he grew up as part of a minority within a minority, namely, the relatively small proportion of gay males who display the effeminate mannerisms of popular caricature. (By contrast, see Chapter 11, dealing with gay police officers, athletes, and politicians who defy the stereotypes.) For Kevyn, hiding the fact that he was "different" was simply not an option. In his hometown of Lafayette, Louisiana, he was incessantly taunted and assaulted by schoolmates for his "sissy" interests and traits. He thought often of killing himself, but could never be certain that local antigay toughs wouldn't beat him to it. After two boys in a pickup truck tried to run him over, he dropped out of high school and moved to Baton Rouge. There, at a store where he was applying for work, he was beaten by a security guard and undercover detectives, apparently for no reason other than his effeminate demeanor. To escape the potentially lethal cultural climate of his home state, he fled to New York City, where the dangers at least were lessened.

There, after some years of struggle, by remaining true to himself and his "sissy" leanings, Kevyn became world renowned as a leader and innovator in the field of fashion and beauty: a makeup artist whose work was the first ever to be featured on nine consecutive *Vogue* covers, the only makeup artist ever to receive an award from the Council of Fashion Designers of America, author of three highly praised books, and a close friend of some of the biggest stars of the entertainment and fashion worlds. His client roster read like a Who's Who of the entertainment world, including scores of stars such as Sharon Stone, Whitney Houston, Cindy Crawford, Cher, and Mary Tyler Moore. His third book alone sold some 400,000 copies.

More importantly, in a world where vanity and shallowness too often reign, Kevyn's personal values remained solid. He never ceased giving his time, energy, and money to worthy causes. He could not erase the image of youngsters growing up gay in Louisiana "with nobody to help them," and he assisted his parents in launching a PFLAG chapter in Lafayette and supported PFLAG nationally in a variety of ways. Within and without the field of fashion, others came to rely on his friendship, strength, and good will. As one book reviewer noted: "While one may puzzle on how it is he finds fulfillment in an industry known for its superficiality and elitism, Aucoin's words are nonetheless infectious and the touches of his brushes inspired."

Looking back on his difficult youth, Kevyn said, "I guess there was one shred of dignity that kept me hanging on, one shred of belief that I was a human being."

Kevyn died prematurely in May 2002, at age forty, of a pituitary brain tumor. He was so beloved by those who had known him, and by the readers of his books, that a year later thousands of tributes were still pouring into his website from around the world. One came from the popular singer Tori Amos: "For those like me who loved Kevyn the person, the heart now weeps. . . . Earth has lost yet another light, but perhaps, he has joined the masters who paint sunsets." Kevyn's mother, Thelma, who with his father Isadore founded that PFLAG chapter in Lafayette, died just a few months after her famous son, in October 2002.

Kevyn's vision was—literally—one of beauty, and he had the courage to remain true to it through the hellish rigors of growing up gay and the potentially character-sapping allurements of the professional world of make-believe.

Jennifer Peters's story reflects both the entrenched quality of homophobia in our schools and some reasons for hope that it nevertheless will ultimately be overcome.

In 2001, Jennifer was nearing the end of her eighth-grade year at Lake Braddock Secondary School in Burke, Virginia, when she experienced something of an epiphany at a commitment ceremony between her aunt and the aunt's life partner. Theretofore oblivious to the existence of the gay minority, she was so touched by the ceremony's aura of love and warmth that she decided then and there, "I need to take a stand for gay and lesbian rights."

On the Internet, she found out about the Gay-Straight Alliance (GSA) initiative. By then, GSAs had been organized at several hundred schools, both to provide support for those students who were gay and to help open and broaden the minds of those who weren't. Just the thing for Lake Braddock, she decided. Early in her freshman year she enlisted a few other interested students, an art professor willing to serve as sponsor, and the support of a wary administration that warned her to be prepared for problems.

She discovered soon enough what they meant. The school P.A. system carried the first announcement of the GSAs formation, and Jennifer likens it to the shot of a starter's gun sending the students on a race to come up with the "best" queer or fag jokes. GSA flyers, simultaneously posted throughout the school, were almost instantaneously ripped down and used as spitballs.

Jennifer herself, moreover, quickly got a taste of what it's like to be part of a minority. Each morning, she found homosexual slurs scribbled on her locker. She was ridiculed for supporting a "Faggot Squad." An opposition flyer announced the formation of a "God Straight Alliance," designed to meet outside the room of any GSA meeting.

But she and her cohorts persevered. They continued their meetings, and the "God Straight Alliance" proved an empty threat. They organized an educational session with faculty department heads, and soon a few teachers began to actively discourage homophobic slurs in the classroom. They hung and re-hung the GSA flyers until finally—success now redefined!—about half would be left hanging.

Then, toward the end of the school year, they proclaimed a "Day of Silence," on which GSA members refrained from speaking throughout the classroom day, and wore T-shirts that explained the silence as a peaceful protest against antigay discrimination. They also readied rainbow ribbons, symbolic of gay equality, for wear by any who might support their cause but would not be willing to be silent all day. Jennifer was delighted when her ribbon supply was exhausted by noon. And an after-school "End the Silence" party drew a significant number of non-GSA members, a clear reflection, to her, of an easing in the school's homophobic atmosphere.

The idea behind GSAs originated with the Gay, Lesbian and Straight Education Network (GLSEN, pronounced "glisten"), which by 2003 pegged the number of gay-straight alliances at schools throughout the country at substantially more than a thousand (more than one hundred in New York alone) and growing rapidly.

An important part of the good news is that many of them are fueled by the energies of heterosexual youths such as Jennifer, fired by a passion for more decent treatment of those who happen to be different from, but no less human than, themselves.

Unfortunately, as noted earlier, in most schools in most parts of the country, GSAs remain unthinkable. "Faggot" remains the put-down of choice. Most gay teachers remain in the closet, anathema to parents and administrators who fear that exposure to homosexuals can somehow turn straight children gay, or that most gays are sexual predators. (In fact, police statistics reveal that approximately ninety-five percent of all convicted sexual abusers of children are heterosexual, suggesting that gays actually commit fewer than their statistical share of such molestation.)

Ostrich like, society insistently refuses to accept a realistic, common-sense approach to homosexuality based on objective fact. Instead, it tacitly promotes the grief, despair, dissolution, and death bred by myth and superstition. The misery will continue until more educators, pediatricians, and politicians are willing to speak out about what many of them know but fear to say: that there will always be a significant minority of our children who are gay, no matter what anybody says or does. Ideally, they would also say what Dr. Spock's presence at that 1972 march suggests he obviously knew then—but which editions of his vastly influential volume on child-rearing never acknowledged until decades later, after his 1998 death.

It is that children can be both gay and OK.

6

Families Under Siege

Bitter statewide electoral fights have left a permanent imprint on families with gay children in two states. And their experiences stand as a warning to all such families everywhere of the incipient cruelty that lurks in the hatred and fear that often masquerades as well-meaning righteousness.

After visiting Colorado Springs in 1892, Katharine Lee Bates wrote the text of the national hymn "America the Beautiful." Millions of visitors there have since been similarly awestruck by the blue-skied grandeur of Pikes Peak and the Rockies' magnificent Front Range.

A century later, however, Bates would no longer have felt comfortable in that land of purple mountains' majesty. A Wellesley College professor of English literature, Bates was also a lesbian. (Which she apparently realized very early: at age nine, she wrote in her diary, "I like women better than men.") And in 1992 in Colorado Springs, at the foot of Pikes Peak, the amber grain was blown by winds of zealous antigay hatred. The fruited plain had become what leaders of an extremist movement centered there liked to call "Ground Zero for the

War between God and Satan," with gay men and lesbians cast in the role of The Devil.

Dozens of fundamentalist ministries headquartered in Colorado Springs joined forces to sponsor a ballot initiative, approved by Colorado voters that year, that would have prohibited laws protecting gays from discrimination.

Four years later, the United States Supreme Court would strike down the provision, known as Amendment Two, as itself amounting to unconstitutional discrimination.

Meanwhile, however, the hate rhetoric spawned by Amendment Two and a similar but even harsher measure in Oregon threatened the composure and very safety of families with gay children in the two states.

In Colorado Springs, devoted Christians Bonnie and Buzz Frum attended the same church as their personal friend and Amendment Two spark plug Will Perkins, head of the smugly christened Coloradoans for Family Values—but were driven out of the church and into anti-Two activism by its members' scornful denunciation of their two gay children.

In Denver, the mother of a gay son, Pat Romero, was waving a "No on 2" sign during rush hour when a driver skidded to a stop, spat on her, and shouted, "Fuck you, dyke!"—an experience she says brought home for her "the terror our children face."

But the 1992 hate initiative crisis was nowhere more dramatically demonstrated than in a small Oregon town, where a physician and his Girl Scout director wife, parents of a lesbian daughter, felt compelled for the first time in their lives to keep a loaded gun in their house.

Jim and Elise Self lived quietly in Grants Pass, Oregon, a small lumber and farming town of about eighteen thousand souls, until the extremists converted the Selfs into reluctant activists.

Jim and Elise, a preschool teacher, had been high school sweethearts in Raleigh, North Carolina. Although their conservative Southern upbringing helped them fit in to small-town life when they moved to Grants Pass in 1977, the Selfs were initially attracted to the area in part because of the easygoing cultural climate that prevailed then. As the seat of Josephine County, located in the Rogue River Valley, one of the country's premier white-water locales, the town had long been a recreation mecca for rafters, canoers, and kayakers. The area was then also known as "Easy Valley" because of its perceived live-and-let-live attitude. Hippie communes were common there in the 1960s and 1970s, and as Jim says, "It was just a place where everybody came and did their own thing."

During the 1980s, however, moral rigidity set in. By 1991, Josephine County counted more than fifty conservative churches devoted to a staunchly patriarchal tradition.

Despite the changing atmosphere, the Selfs flourished in Grants Pass. They raised two gifted and popular children, Robert and Jennifer. Their lives centered on their careers, their friends, and the education and extracurricular activities of their children. Jim and Elise were prime movers in the PTA and in the Boosters Club. Jim served as volunteer physician for the high school football team, and Elise was a director of the five-county Winema Council of the Girl Scouts of America. The family often spent weekends and vacations camping and canoeing through the mountains and beaches of the Pacific Northwest.

In short, the Selfs were pillars of conventionality in a locale where supporting gay rights could in the best of times threaten careers and friendships and evoke social ostracism. And 1991—when the Selfs learned their daughter Jennifer was gay—was not the best of times in Oregon. It was the year in which an ugly cloud of bigotry and violence was descending over the state. And the cloud was darkest in rural areas such as Grants Pass.

An important influence in the rightward shift in Grants Pass was the founding in the 1980s of the Oregon Citizens Alliance (OCA), a religion-oriented spin-off of the Oregon Republican Party. The OCA scored its first major triumph in 1988, when it sponsored an initiative that overturned an executive order banning discrimination in state hiring based on sexual orientation. In 1991, the organization found its full homophobic voice when it launched a petition drive promoting what would become Ballot Measure Nine.

The OCA collected the necessary signatures, and its measure was placed on the 1992 general ballot. Number Nine did not simply call for the repeal of existing gay-rights ordinances in three cities and the banning of their adoption elsewhere in the state; it equated gayness with pedophilia, sadism, and masochism. If passed, it would establish as a constitutional tenet—and as required teaching in all the state's public schools and colleges—that homosexuality is "abnormal, wrong, unnatural, and perverse." Besides the personal threat to his family, Jim worried with other physicians that the University of Oregon School of Medicine could lose its accreditation because of its failure to teach that homosexuality was perverse.

Jennifer's disclosure led Jim and Elise to join a hardy band of vastly outnumbered PFLAG families who actively opposed Number Nine in the rural areas of Oregon. They spoke at community meetings, appeared on radio and television talk shows, handed out literature, and registered voters. They also put up with personal abuse. In nearby Ashland, a telephone caller told PFLAGer Chuck Steele, "Wouldn't it be nice if all homosexuals were dead?" Another phoned the Steeles' friend and fellow PFLAGer, Gerry Garland, to say, "You ought to be ashamed to have a fucking queer son." Moments after Garland hung up, the same man called back. "I forgot," he said. "Does the bastard have AIDS yet?"

The worst tragedy occurred in Salem, where a lesbian and a gay man were burned to death in an arson incident apparently triggered by campaign emotions. In Portland, the "No on Nine" offices were burglarized and vandalized, and mailing lists were destroyed.

Portland Police Chief Tom Potter minimized the mayhem by assigning special units to prevent violence from either side. Potter was already a pet whipping boy of the Radical Right because he supported his lesbian daughter, who was an officer on his force, and because he recruited other gay and lesbian officers. (See Chapter Seven.) His efforts to calm the situation prompted death threats and calls for his resignation.

The Selfs, after receiving a number of angry letters, for the first time kept a loaded gun in the house. "I was that scared," Jim says. At times, he said, it seemed as though "an atmosphere of total fear" had descended on the gay community and its supporters. So it was that in little Grants Pass, amid the spectacular beauty of the Rogue River Valley, the Self family found themselves caught in a hurricane of hate. And so it is that their story differs so strikingly from that of those of us who risk little or nothing by supporting our gay children. Theirs is truly a story of high courage. It is a tale of genuine family values—a blend of personal integrity, compassion, pride, and faith in one another—that withstood the gales of hostility and ignorance loosed by moral fervor gone wild.

Jennifer Self was one of North Valley High's all-time outstanding scholar-athletes. While racking up the grades that made her class valedictorian, she was an all-state performer in basketball, volleyball, and softball. She was a two-time participant in a prestigious local scholastic competition known as the Academic Masters contest, and she won its top honors in English. She won a free-ride basketball scholarship to the University of California at Berkeley. There, while earning admission to a national honor society for psychology majors, she twice broke the school's season record for three-point shots. She is well known and, at least until 1992, was highly regarded throughout Grants Pass and Josephine County. To her family, as Elise says, "she is warm and caring and sensitive and vulnerable and angry and sad, funny and human."

Of herself, however, Jennifer has written, "All those years I was growing up in Grants Pass and passing as the straight-laced-goody-two-shoes-heterosexual-egghead-jock, I was living in sadness and fear of what would happen if everyone around me knew my secret. I was and am a gay woman . . .

"There I was, a teenager, knowing that I felt the same pains, heard the same music, loved the same loves, and cried the same tears as all of my 'straight' friends. And yet I was receiving messages from society that I was not normal, not OK." After Jennifer moved to Berkeley, Jim and Elise would often drive six hours to watch her play basketball, say hello for a little while, and then drive home. But even on these short visits, they sensed something amiss.

"A wall seemed to have grown between us," says Elise. "We'd go down there and then wouldn't have anything to talk to her about. And the phone calls were really excruciating. 'Hi, Mom and Dad, it's Jennifer'—and then, nothing. We felt we had to carry the whole load of the conversation, that we had to do all the talking."

During those excruciating silences, Jennifer was often silently mouthing into the telephone, "I'm gay, I'm gay." But she couldn't say it out loud except to her brother, Robert, then attending Oregon State University in Corvallis. Nevertheless, Jim and Elise were beginning to suspect the source of the unease. Jennifer had come out to most of her acquaintances on campus, and the Selfs noticed unmistakable signs when they visited.

"In a way," Elise says, "Jennifer did nothing to hide it." At the games it seemed there was "always a group of women around her." She lived with some other women in a house, and Elise recalls that at one point, "there was some kind of big split-up—two of them had to get out of the house real quick, almost like a lovers' quarrel."

Finally, the parents asked Robert whether he thought Jennifer might be gay. Robert, respecting his sister's request for confidentiality, told them to ask Jennifer directly. Elise remembers the scene:

"It was after her sophomore year. We were all together, the four of us, and we sat her down in the family room. I said, 'Jennifer, there's a wall between us. Is there anything you want to tell us?' She said, 'No.' I said, 'Do you want me to make it easy for you?' She said, 'Yes.' I said, 'Are you gay?' She said, 'Yes.'

"And the wall came tumbling down. It was such a relief to have that secret out of the way. We cried. Then we could start dealing with all the feelings."

After what Elise describes as that "wonderful talk," however, the information was slow to extend beyond the family.

"I'm not proud to admit it," Elise says, "but quite frankly, my biggest concern at first, other than worry about Jennifer and her life, was, 'What are people going to think? What's my family going to think?'"

Then, by chance, Elise found PFLAG.

While visiting Robert during "Mom's Weekend" at OSU in the spring of his senior year, Elise saw a sign announcing a meeting of the Corvallis PFLAG group in a campus building. She grabbed Robert's hand and ran up the stairs and joined the meeting. For the first time, Elise was talking about Jennifer's gayness to people outside her immediate family.

"I cried and cried," she says. "It was the first time I had been with a group of people where I felt I could open up and talk about my daughter in a proud way, and be heard and be understood. It was a marvelous feeling."

Before she left the meeting, the leader gave her Candace Steele's phone number. Back home, Elise timidly dialed the number and Candace answered.

"I could barely get it out," Elise says with a laugh. "Finally, I said it. 'I have a lesbian daughter.' And she said, 'Well, I have two lesbian daughters.' So it was wonderful."

Elise and Jim attended several PFLAG meetings in Ashland. They had assumed that they were the only people in Grants Pass with a gay child—or who even knew anybody gay. But Candace gave them the names of gay and lesbian contacts there, and urged them to start a local PFLAG group. The Selfs agreed to make an attempt and planned a meeting in their home. Publicity was strictly by word of mouth, but, to their surprise, ten people showed up. They continued to hold monthly meetings, and a year and a half later, the average attendance had grown to about twenty-five. "We've heard that gay people are everywhere," Jim said. "And if we could draw that many family members to PFLAG meetings in a place like Grants Pass, I've got to believe it."

At the first meeting the Selfs had attended in Ashland, Jim had solemnly announced that he would never become an activist. But about the time the Selfs were hosting their first meeting, the OCA qualified their hate-ridden initiative for the ballot.

"Can you imagine it?" Jim asks. "You have just had your daughter come out to you, and then you sit and read that these people are lumping her with pedophiles and sadists. We were absolutely horrified. So all of a sudden, my resolve not to become an activist went into the trash can. We simply could not sit still and watch this hate campaign against people we loved."

For starters, Elise helped form a local human-rights alliance that attracted a number of prominent local citizens and bridged the gap between the gay and non-gay communities. The alliance had been the dream of a group of closeted lesbians for whom the encouragement of a non-gay person provided the necessary impetus to make it a reality. The first meeting attracted eighty people—what Elise calls "a *very* large turnout for our little town." Nor was the meeting without drama. As Elise tells it:

"Jim and I stood up and came out publicly for the first time before so many local people. Then we went around the room. And every one of those eighty people shared some story about prejudice or discrimination they had experienced in their lives—because they were Jewish, or Catholic, or a person of color, or gay, or whatever. It was an incredible evening. It was a very intimate evening with eighty people, if you can imagine that. We never dreamed we could have an experience like that in Grants Pass."

The Selfs were proud of their role in creating this group to oppose the OCA, but they could not yet imagine coming out to the town as a whole. They even asked the meeting participants not to disclose Jennifer's secret. Jim's eighty-three-year-old mother also lived in Grants Pass, and they hadn't even told her.

"So you can see how scared we still were," Elise says. As Jim notes, however, "The pressure was really mounting now. We've got my mother in town, and Elise's parents back East who don't know, but we're also feeling an incredible urgency to get this message out, and to get out in the streets and start fighting the OCA."

The final push out of the closet was a call from Candace Steele. Opponents of Number Nine were putting together a voters' pamphlet that would include the names of PFLAG parents. Would the Selfs allow their names to be used? Undecided, Jim and Elise called Jennifer in Berkeley.

"If you're ready to come out, I'm ready to have my name out there," was Jennifer's reply. "We need to fight this."

It was a momentous decision. For the first time, they would be out—not only in town, but statewide. "This was bigger than Grants Pass," Elise says. "But we said yes."

Now they had to inform the grandparents. They first told Jim's mother, Roberta Self. Jennifer couldn't get away from school to do it in person, but she nervously instructed her parents, "Ask Grandma if I still get the dishes."

She needn't have worried. Roberta Self's first reaction surprised and amused Jim and Elise. "Well," she snorted, "I feel better about the situation now. She's not down there on campus with those boys pawing all over her."

Next, the Selfs sent separate letters, one from Elise and Jim and one from Jennifer, to Elise's parents. Jennifer told her grandparents, "I am giving you a gift, and the gift is me and who I am."

"My folks called right away," Elise says. "My father left a message on the machine saying, 'We are with you. We read your letters several times. We have cried, and we love you and we love Jennifer.'

"But it hasn't been easy for them. They love Jennifer very much. They don't blame anyone. They understand that this is not a choice. But they have all that social conditioning we all have and they have to deal with that."

The Selfs' first live "media event" was a candlelight vigil for human rights on the steps of the county courthouse. Jim can now laugh at the fact that the report of his first public statement in support of gay rights, printed in the next day's newspaper, made it appear that he himself was gay: "I am only now learning how difficult it is to be openly gay in a heterosexual society."

But it was Elise who provided the emotional highlight of the evening. In proud and defiant tones, she read her personal tribute to her daughter:

She cannot be reduced to statistics, polls, stereotypes, nicknames,
    prejudice, opinion.
She is my child.
I still have the same dreams. The details may have changed, but
    the dreams are the same:
Of happiness, love, home, family, meaningful work.
Because, you see, she is my child.
She's not some monster to be feared, some pervert to be sneered at,
    some child molester or converter of adolescents.
She is my child.

She is warm and caring and sensitive and vulnerable and angry
and sad, funny and human.

Yes, she is my child.

She didn't drop from another planet to cause destruction and
mayhem.

She came from love between her father and me.

Yes, she is my child.

You will not harm her if I can prevent it. You will not hurt her.

She is my child.

I join with every black mother, every Jewish mother, every Native
American mother, every Hispanic mother, every Asian mother,
every disabled child's mother, every gay child's mother, and
every mother whose child has known hatred and prejudice.

And I say they are our children, our very special, precious children.

But even as Elise's words stirred the hearts of those at the vigil, the vicious OCA campaign continued to pound away at them. "Every single day we picked up the newspaper and read in effect about what a pervert our child was," Elise remembers. "It is difficult to convey the level of fear, of sheer intimidation, that the OCA's campaign had created."

Nevertheless, when a lesbian friend arranged for an interview by the Grants Pass *Daily Courier* with some gay residents, Jim and Elise agreed to join them. It was an opportunity to bring their family perspective more directly to the local townspeople. So, warily—uncertain what the tenor of the article might be—they endorsed the newspaper's plan to include a story about them in a series on Number Nine.

On the morning the article was to appear, Jim and Elise awakened together, in near panic, at 4 A.M. They sat rigidly in their living room, waiting for daybreak. Jim broke the tension—"Do you think we could go buy every *Courier* in town?" Eventually, they reassured themselves with the thought that the story would probably be buried on the community pages.

But when the *Courier* came out that afternoon, a huge picture of Elise, Jennifer, and Jim in a grinning, three-way embrace—with Elise sporting a T-shirt reading "Straight but Not Narrow"—loomed from every newsstand in town. "Local Family Loves Its Lesbian Daughter" blared the front-page banner above the picture.

The story was positive. It described the Selfs as "an all-American family sparked by high achievement." It contrasted Jennifer's public stardom with the inner tumult of her high school years, and told of the difficult experience of coming out to her family and the ensuing family closeness. It described the Selfs' PFLAG experience. It quoted Robert saying of his parents, "I'm proud of them." And it concluded with a quote from Jim: "People who have gays or lesbians in their family do believe in traditional values. They do love their families."

The article infuriated local members of the OCA, and for two weeks, the *Courier* was picketed by protesters complaining that the newspaper was unfair to the organization.

"Can you believe it?" Jim still marvels. "They turned *themselves* into the victims! They said they were being discriminated against because the newspaper had the nerve to print this story. I'm not sure what they wanted. Maybe a story about people who *didn't* love their daughter?"

The article also triggered heavy response from across the political and religious spectrums. The *Courier* received waves of letters to the editor and the Selfs were deluged with telephone calls, letters, and comments from passersby.

Many of the responses were angry and vicious. The Selfs received a spate of hate letters, and it was the edge-of-violence tone of many of them that led Jim to get a gun. And the virulence of the OCA campaign seemed to have no limits. One pro-amendment flier, never renounced by the OCA, actually called for castrating and executing all gays. The "perverted gay lobby will be defeated," it said, "only when all Christians unite" to "implement God's methods to exterminate homosexuals . . . Execution . . . Castration . . . Imprisonment."

But there were compensations. For months after the article was published, people stopped the Selfs on the street to tell them, "Thanks for the article; I have someone gay in my family." Nearly a year later, addressing delegates to a national PFLAG convention, Jim choked back tears as he read a letter that the family had received in 1992. It was from Lorenz "Lefty" Schultz, pastor of Newman Church, and more than one hundred members of the congregation.

Dear Jim, Elise, and Jennifer,

In the past couple of years, you and your family have been through an extraordinary journey together. In the interest of creating a human community where understanding, compassion, and tolerance can abide instead of intolerance and fear, you have taken some very great risks in sharing your story with the whole community. We suspect that your willingness to share such depth and vulnerability may have exposed you to the hatred and bigotry that represents a darker side of our community.

As a congregation, we are not all of a single mind on the issue of homosexuality; but in our differences we can unite in affirming the importance of communication, caring love, growth, truth-telling, the ability to rejoice in laughter, and to share the wellspring of tears and fundamental values which lie at the heart of deep and precious family relationships.

We hear much rhetoric these days about family values and family relationships. You and your family live and embody those family values.

As members and friends of Newman Church, we reach out to you in love and caring. You need to know that you represent the best that we have to offer this community. We are pleased to call you neighbors and friends.

During the frenzied final weeks of the campaign, hundreds of advertisements were placed in the *Courier* by both sides of the Number Nine controversy. On the final weekend before the vote, one full-page ad featured a letter from Jennifer addressed "Dear Citizens of Josephine County." In it, she recounted her youthful years in Grants Pass, described the hardship created by negative public attitudes toward homosexuality, and pleaded for understanding and tolerance.

She realized, she wrote, that many people held religious beliefs that prevented them from accepting homosexuality. But to those, she said, "I pose the question, what's the danger, the evil, in accepting and loving someone you don't understand or agree with? Aren't these the ideals by which Jesus Christ lived life?" She urged them, "Make a vote for love, acceptance, and education, and vote no on Ballot Measure Nine."

Significantly, and probably crucially, similar pleas were being made by numerous non-fundamentalist churches. The Ecumenical Ministries of Oregon, representing seventeen denominations and more than two thousand congregations, correctly described the initiative as promoting "a climate of bigotry, hatred, and intimidation." And in what many considered a landmark event, Oregon's Catholic bishops joined the "No on Nine" forces, denouncing the measure as "potentially harmful and discriminatory."

On election day, Number Nine was defeated fifty-seven to forty-three percent. In Portland, three thousand people at a post-election rally gave a rousing ovation to PFLAGer Marge Work, a tireless "No on Nine" campaigner. Presented with a certificate from the gay community designating her as "our PFLAG Mom for loving us unconditionally," she told the crowd, "It's a mother's prerogative to brag about her children. You've honored me with the title, so I'm going to claim the prerogative. I'm so proud of you, every one of you. You're fine the way you are. You are loved. And we are here for you."

Amendment Nine's defeat relied heavily, however, on its overwhelming opposition in Portland. Rural counties approved of the measure by resounding margins that ran as high as two to one.

In Grants Pass, the statewide win was bittersweet. In Josephine County, fifty-eight percent of the voters endorsed the measure.

The OCA was heartened by the amendment's heavy support in rural areas, as well as by the success of Colorado's Amendment Two the same day. So, within months, the OCA was sponsoring "Baby Number Nine's"—local ordinances banning civil-rights protections for gays—in the twenty counties that had favored the statewide measure. One of them became Proposition 17-1 on Josephine County's 1993 primary ballot; the Selfs once again found themselves in electoral battle.

Two months before the election, the entire family took a well-earned breather; they joined some 2,000 PFLAG members and an estimated 750,000 others in a massive turnout for the 1993 march on Washington for gay rights. When Jim and Elise returned to face the

Proposition 17-1 campaign, they wrote an op-ed piece for the *Courier*; it described their "inspirational and emotional weekend" in Washington and drew lessons for the voters of Josephine County.

They had cried, they wrote, when they stood before the Lincoln Memorial and read Lincoln's words about a nation "dedicated to the proposition that all men are created equal." They cried again when they walked along the Vietnam War Memorial, read the names of Americans killed, and wondered which of them were gay men or lesbians. And they cried yet again, they wrote, at the new Holocaust Memorial Museum (see Chapter 12): "It was not insignificant that the Museum opened at the time of the march. It was chilling to remember what the Nazis did to gays and lesbians, while at the same time reading the signs of some who came to protest the March: DEATH TO ALL FAGS!"

It was also during the final weeks of the Proposition 17-1 campaign that Jennifer received from her grandmother a gift more valuable by far than the family dishes. A letter penned and signed by Roberta Self in her precise handwriting was mailed to fifteen thousand Josephine County voters. In it, after declaring her love for her granddaughter, she wrote, "What they [the OCA] are really doing is trying to hurt my grand-daughter. They are trying to hurt so many of our precious children."

The letter became known throughout the county as "the grand-mother letter." Jim says, "So here's my eighty-three-year-old Southern Baptist, prim, proper, Virginian mother, who prides herself on being a very private person, now being a community celebrity. For about ten days, she was absolutely deluged with telephone calls." Newspapers ran stories about Roberta Self and her letter, and it was the topic of a heated two-hour discussion on a local fundamentalist radio talk show.

One columnist wrote about the "swarm of angry phone calls"

Roberta had received from Bible-quoting critics, and lauded her calm response. "Her well-worn Bible speaks of a God of understanding and compassion for all, not one of intolerance and hatred to those who may be different," he wrote. "Our world needs more such grandmothers."

Still, the Self family message was no match for ingrained stereotypes and the slick, moneyed campaign of the antigay forces. On June 28, 1993, Proposition 17-1 passed by an overwhelming margin.

Elise, drawing an analogy to the Rogue River, says that in the family's journey in support of their daughter, "We have hit white water—and it can be scary." But they paddle on because, as Elise puts it, "We now know that there are people on the banks cheering us on. And there are a lot of others who have taken to their boats and gotten in the river with us. So we feel a lot safer now because we know we're not alone."

Moreover, she says, the journey has been "an incredibly liberating experience" for the entire family. "Coming out has been an enormous relief. I feel so free. I don't care anymore what anybody else might think."

That, it seems, is one of the rewards of true courage.

Meanwhile, in Colorado, boosted by a landslide two-to-one "yes" vote in Colorado Springs, Amendment Two passed statewide by 53 to 47 percent. Its supporters cheered, but the state's citizens soon had cause to question the wisdom of their vote. The day after the election, a protest march of seven thousand people in Denver was led by both Colorado Governor Roy Romer and Denver Mayor Wellington Webb. On the same day, the American Association of Physicians for Human Rights canceled its convention in Denver. Colorado sported a new nickname: "The Hate

State," and a national Boycott Colorado movement gained momentum. Tourist and convention trade declined: the Atlanta City Council, for example, banned city employees from traveling to, or spending money in, Colorado. And the ultimately successful legal challenge to Amendment Two was filed by the cities of Denver, Boulder, and Aspen, and by several individuals, including tennis star and Aspen resident Martina Navratilova.

In the election aftermath, Bonnie and Buzz Frum spent a few hours in their living room sharing views with old friend and Amendment Two spark plug Will Perkins. "We tried to help him see he didn't have a corner on the market as to a Christian perspective on sexuality," Buzz reported. They told Perkins in particular that they resented the attempt by the amendment's backers to usurp the "family values" banner. They said they were honoring the family values they grew up with in their own traditional families: love, respect, compassion, integrity, and mutual support.

Perkins in turn told them he regretted the choice of his organization's name, Coloradoans for Family Values, because he realized that others, such as the Frums, were also family-oriented. But ten years later he obviously remained as firm as ever in his antigay passion: a Denver newspaper's 2002 review of the long-term effect of Amendment Two quoted Perkins as saying he would, "in a heartbeat," sponsor a similar movement again.

The Colorado campaign, by putting parents on notice about the genuine threats to their children, triggered a substantial growth in PFLAG membership and activity. Chapters throughout the state reported swelling attendance and membership. In Colorado Springs, where the Frums became co-presidents in early 1993, average meeting attendance grew fourfold in the first few months after the election. Nevertheless, for some years, the charged local atmosphere prevented advertising the meetings' location. "We didn't want to take a chance on parents being accosted going to meetings," Bonnie explained.

Katharine Lee Bates was a talented lesbian with an artistic soul that spawned a national hymn with its vision of American grandeur. A century after composing her most famous work, she presumably would have been proud of all those like the Frums who defended basic human rights in the land of spacious skies and purple mountains' majesty.

7

Parents Speak Out: The Surgeon and the Supercop

Plainly, most parents of gay children, do not become activists. But many do. And, for sheer drama, the stories of two fathers, recounted below, stand out—both of them set largely in an era a decade and more ago, when antigay attitudes were even more pervasive and virulent than they are now. One of the fathers was an orthopedic surgeon and national power-lifting champion who vainly pleaded with his Navy flier son not to go public about his homosexuality, but soon found himself in the media glare, at his son's side, before a Navy review board. The other, a nationally respected chief of police, willingly risked his prestige—but saw it in fact grow—when he actively supported his gay constituents and a lesbian police officer who happened to be his own daughter.

Meanwhile, in more mundane ways, thousands of other parents strive daily to relieve society's unfair treatment of the children they love. They do it, largely without fanfare, in a variety of forums: in their churches, in private meetings with municipal and school officials, before school boards and city councils, in state capitals, and on Capitol Hill. They appear on radio and television talk shows, write letters to newspapers, meet with local media managers, and are frequent subjects of magazine and newspaper features.

Perhaps their most important work will turn out to be with our nation's schools and churches, where lifelong attitudes and biases are formed and solidified. Parents of gay children regularly help organize conferences where teachers can gain continuing-education credit for learning more about the problems of gay youth; work to place books helpful to both teachers and students in school libraries; and pressure school boards to adopt—and more importantly, enforce—antidiscrimination policies. In their churches, parents of gay children have been among the leaders in virtually every denomination to urge more humane attitudes toward a substantial minority in their congregations.

Every such parent can take inspiration from the surgeon and the supercop.

The Surgeon

Pat Thorne says her youngest child, Tracy, differed from her other two in one notable respect.

"When his brother and sister were little, if somebody spilled something on the floor, and I'd say, 'Who did this?' they'd say, 'Not me.' Tracy was different. He'd say, 'I did.' That's just the way he was.

"He'd always tell you whatever was on his mind. At times, I wished he'd be more tactful."

Tracy was also bright, gregarious, and a natural leader. In high school, he was president of several organizations while lettering in cross-country and serving as the manager of the football team. At Vanderbilt University, he was a member of the executive committee of his fraternity for three years, and its president when he was a senior.

Pat's concern about Tracy's frankness resurfaced late in his senior year, when an exhilarated Tracy gathered the family together to announce he had decided to join the Navy. "I could see he was really excited about the Navy. But I wondered if he could take orders without telling his superiors whatever he might be thinking," she recalls.

For four years, it appeared as though her worries were groundless. Tracy's Navy career soared.

When he decided to enlist, he was still a political science major at Vanderbilt. But a week after graduation, he joined seventy-one other officer candidates at Pensacola Naval Air Station. Four months later, he was commissioned an ensign, completing officer training with out-standing achievement awards in both academics and physical training.

But greater distinctions were to come, first in flight training and later as a bombardier/navigator in an elite squadron known as the "Flying Tigers." In four separate phases of his flight training, Tracy finished first in his class, winning "Top Gun" honors as the outstanding student of the year. As a Flying Tiger, he received the highest perform-ance ratings possible. On two occasions, he was selected as one of only two officers to receive special leadership training. He would later be publicly described by a fellow flier as "one of the finest Navy officers I've ever met." And the captain who pinned on his wings said he hoped Tracy would someday command the Navy.

But the stubborn streak of honesty caught up with Tracy in 1992 when, for the first time in his life, he fell in love—with a man.

At five feet nine inches tall and 175 pounds, the ruggedly hand-some Tracy strikes a macho image that could easily have camouflaged his gayness and protected his career indefinitely. But he could not, as it were, fly under false colors. He loved the Navy, and accepted its word regarding the qualities—honesty, integrity, loyalty to self—it purported to honor in its officers. Lieutenant Thorne sent his commanding officer a letter saying he was about to announce his homosexuality to Ted Koppel on *Nightline*.

In college, Tracy had been the only fraternity president to attend meetings about improving conditions for minority students. Now he was ready to stand up for fair play for another minority—his own. He had agreed to go on *Nightline*, he wrote his commanding officer, because he had come to "feel strongly that the Navy's current policy toward homosexuals is unfair."

That night, he said essentially the same thing to a national audience. The next day, members of his squadron—including the commanding officer—expressed support for his courage. But higher up the chain of command, the reaction was swift and hostile. Within two days, Tracy's name was scraped from his A-6 Intruder attack jet, he was detached from his squadron, and discharge proceedings were begun.

On July 23, 1992, a three-officer board of review convened at Oceana Naval Air Station in Virginia Beach to consider the case. Some two dozen correspondents jostled in the cramped hearing room to report on what amounted to a fait accompli. Tracy's lawyer offered seventy-nine witnesses and exhibits that were ruled irrelevant and inadmissible. The proffered witnesses included Dr. Lawrence J. Korb, former assistant secretary of defense in the Reagan administration; according to Tracy's lawyer, Korb would have testified that retaining Tracy would not be incompatible with the military mission.

To the board, however, the sole relevant evidence consisted of videotapes from *Nightline*, *The Today Show*, and a CNN talk show on which Tracy had said he was gay. The Navy had spent some $2 million to train a Top Gun, but under prevailing regulations, his statements on television were deemed sufficient cause to squander superstar talent and substantial taxpayer investment. The board's recommendation to discharge Tracy was foreordained.

But if the three officers were unanimously hostile, Tracy was buoyed by the presence of three civilians who were equally unwavering in their support. They were his parents, Roscoe and Pat, and his sister, Patricia.

The appearance of Roscoe, a West Palm Beach orthopedic surgeon, was a surprise to even the other Thornes. He had objected to Tracy appearing on *Nightline*, and had declined to accompany his wife and daughter when they left home for the hearing. But later, he apparently had a sort of epiphany born of weeks of intensive self-examination. On the second afternoon of the hearing, he strode purposefully into the room and asked to address the panel.

His mere appearance was poignant to his family, and his subsequent impassioned plea to the board provided the dramatic highlight of the hearing. It would spawn articles about him in scores of publications, from the *Miami Herald* to *Harper's* magazine, throughout the country.

In fact, Roscoe came across more as a lumberjack or oil-field roustabout than as a physician. Years of pumping iron formed his 235 pounds into mounds of sculptured muscle that rippled over his six-foot frame. Massive shoulders and beefy jowls appeared to meet over the slightest hint of neck. A curly bush of dark brown hair framed a brooding bulldog face that rarely relaxed its scowling intensity.

In 1991, Roscoe dead-lifted 525 pounds in the course of becoming the nation's power-lifting champion for men in his weight class over the age of forty. Roscoe was sixty-one.

He spoke, even in ordinary conversation, with the same single-minded intensity he brought to pressing iron. He did not suffer fools gladly, and his tone sometimes suggested that the category was reserved primarily for those who differed with his views. He disliked confrontation, and needed to feel in control of his surroundings.

So it's not surprising that he was reluctant to talk about the two-month period between learning he had a gay son and his appearance at Tracy's discharge hearing. It was a time when certainty and control must have seemed elusive, a time of dreaded ambivalence, when fixed beliefs clashed with protective parental instincts.

Tracy had come out to his mother and sister in 1991, confident of their support, just months after he had fully acknowledged his homosexuality to himself. But he had delayed telling his father until he was compelled to do so by his decision to go on *Nightline*.

Tracy says his father took the news very badly. He urged Tracy to get a cure through psychiatric treatment, or at least to marry and have children anyway. He adamantly opposed Tracy's planned television appearance. "This doesn't have to leave this room," he pleaded.

While Roscoe shied from discussing his thoughts or feelings during the next months, he plainly was severely distressed. He became uncharacteristically subdued. He refused to watch Tracy on *Nightline*. He sank into an emotional funk that led a colleague to recommend he take a break from his medical practice. He told his family to go to the Virginia Beach hearing without him.

Then, his doubts appear suddenly to have coalesced into powerful conviction. The day before the hearing, Tracy found a message from his father on his answering machine: "I'm coming up. If a father can't stick up for his son, he isn't worth having as a father."

Roscoe hurriedly packed, rushed to the airport, fueled up his private Navajo aircraft, and took off for Virginia Beach. It was only when in the air, he later told Tracy, that he thought about what he wanted to say to the board of review.

In the hearing room, he first listened intently as Tracy made his statement to the panel: "This policy is in complete contradiction to the qualities of a leader the Navy advances . . . if I cannot be honest with myself, if I cannot respect myself, how can I expect others to respect me?" Looking directly at the three officers, Tracy said, "You are leaders of men. You are not machines. If you allow yourselves to not question a policy that is based on ancient hatred and bigotry and not based on reality, you are allowing yourselves to be machines."

When Tracy finished, Roscoe was granted permission to address the panel. He spoke for nearly half an hour, emotionally and without notes. His first-ever public speech constituted a powerful commentary on the nature and origins of prejudice.

He began quietly, obviously moved by the words he had just heard from his son, recalling Tracy's birth: "A friend of mine took my wife into the delivery room and I waited outside as a young physician. He came out and handed me a baby boy . . . I put a stethoscope on him, and looked at his arms and his legs, and I thought he was just fine.

"But until I heard this man just now, I didn't realize what a great man was given to me by that doctor friend, delivered to my wife twenty-five years ago."

Then he took the panel to task.

"America, great country that it is, is bleeding because of a lot of wounds, prejudices, that are still left over . . . and you all are here worrying about a twenty-five-year-old man that has already proved himself beyond a shadow of a doubt as a leader, as a commander, as a superb individual.

"I'm happy to say I'm his father and I wish I could be like him. Forgive me for my emotions, but I wish I could be as good a man as Tracy Thorne is."

Out of his weeks of anguished meditation, Roscoe had concluded that his initial reaction to his son's homosexuality had sprung from his own bias. Now, he reviewed the profound effect of prejudice on his own life.

When he was five, he said, he had a black friend named Jesse. "I was so happy to see him one day, I took him by the hand and I took him up to my white mother, and I said, 'Mama, this is Jesse.' . . . My mother was a real kind, good person and she smiled down at Jesse and she said, 'It's nice to meet you, Jesse.'

"Later that day Jesse went home, and my mama came over to me and she said, 'Buddy, you never introduce a colored person to a white lady.' I said, 'Yes, Mama, I won't do that anymore.' I was being trained in Jackson, Mississippi, by a white woman, my mother, who was a good person, but that's the way she was trained and she was passing it along. She was in the dark. She was living in the darkness, with prejudice, and she was passing that education of darkness on to me."

Later, he said, he saw water fountains and restrooms marked "colored" and "white." When he was fourteen, he visited California with his parents and saw a restaurant sign that said, "No Mexicans or colored allowed." "That sounded about right to me," he said. "That's the way I'd been trained. I wasn't a Mexican, I wasn't colored, and I went on in.

"I'm responding as I had been trained in the Deep South of Jackson, Mississippi. I wasn't thinking for myself."

He remembered his mother taking him to a swimming pool on a trip to Illinois, where a "Gentiles only" sign hung over the gate. I said, 'Mama, what is a gentile?' And she said, 'Shut up. You're one.' And I went on in. I didn't know what a gentile was, but I was one of them. So I'm being educated all along."

Later, after serving with the infantry in the Korean War, he enrolled at the University of Mississippi. He said there was only one black man on campus, a blind man who sold pencils in front of the administration building. "Everyone loved 'blind Jim.' He wasn't a threat to anybody. So it didn't make any difference that he was on campus or not, because he didn't threaten anybody."

Then he recalled a memory that plainly still pained him. He was working as a graduate pharmacist in a Jackson drugstore, and a young nurse sat down at the soda fountain.

"She had on a pretty white uniform, and she was a registered nurse, but she was a black person. And my boss nudged me in the ribs and said, 'Roscoe, go over there and run her off.'

"I was twenty-five years old, Tracy's age. And I was intelligent, but I had been trained. And so I went over there, and I said, 'You're going to have to leave. We don't want you in here.' And this young nurse looked at me. She was about my age or maybe a little younger, and she was a registered nurse and a fine-looking human being, and tears ran down her cheeks and she left. And I felt so bad.

"I wonder where she is right now, because she's probably about my age. I know she'd remember. I chased her out of the drugstore."

Later, he said, in medical school, his colleagues included a few light-skinned blacks, but "no real black blacks." He noticed, though, that when bodies were dissected in anatomy class, "they all looked pretty much the same." Still later, the government decreed an end to seg-regation in hospitals. Although he thought it wouldn't work, "We put them together and we treated them. And things were better for it."

In an emotional peroration, he warned the panel members that ruling against Tracy could haunt their consciences: "I want you officers here to know that if you allow anything to happen that would interfere with this young man's ability to have his freedom to serve his country as he so ably proved his ability to do . . . then when you go home tonight, I want each of you to find a good friend. I want you to sit down with that good friend, and I want you to tell him what you allowed to happen."

In the hallway after the hearing, both in tears, Roscoe and Tracy embraced.

"We've got to stop this pain, son," said Roscoe.

Eighteen months later, Roscoe still refused to talk about the weeks that followed Tracy's coming out. Queried directly about that painful time, he told a newspaper reporter he wouldn't have agreed to an inter-view if he had known he would be asked to "elaborate on me." He would say only, "Any change causes adjustments . . . and sixty-year-old men don't like to make adjustments, but we have to sometimes, and we're willing to."

About that time, I visited Roscoe and Pat in their comfortable West Palm Beach home. I asked Roscoe what had gone on in his mind during that time directly before the hearing, but he would say only that he thought the decision "was instinctive rather than anything else." Parents "always come to the defense of their children, especially if they've been falsely accused or deprived of their rights. That was an instinctive act."

Perhaps, I thought, he simply was reluctant to admit to ever having had feelings that in hindsight seemed to him to be wrong. Or perhaps, like so many other Americans, he was not yet wholly comfortable with the notion of homosexuality itself.

And, indeed, his attitude in this regard posed something of an anomaly. The man who spoke so eloquently on behalf of his gay son, it turned out, was uneasy with the movement for gay civil rights. At first, he hesitated even to talk to me because he resented the name of an organization, PFLAG, to which I was clearly devoted. Although Pat had had some involvement with PFLAG, Roscoe had resisted. "I don't like your using the term 'gays and lesbians,'" he said. It is simply wrong, he said, his voice rising, to describe a human being by some single characteristic such as sexual orientation. "You might as well say this man with ingrown toenails, let's put him over here in this category. And, you know, there are some peculiar ones that I'm really watching, and that's those left-handed ingrates. They are a group, and it's time we get some laws passed."

He paused, then spluttered, "Ignorance! We're all just human beings, that's all."

Ironically, the son he so admired was an active spokesman for a movement he apparently resented. And it's a movement, of course, with the ultimate aim of putting itself out of business by making homosexuality a no more significant personal characteristic than ingrown toenails or left-handedness.

During the intense national debate over gays in the military in 1993, Tracy became a national leader in the campaign for a policy of integration. His classic Norman Rockwell, all-American charisma automatically cast him as a natural spokesman for the cause; he appeared on numerous leading talk shows and before various congressional committees. He debated admirals and senators and others, coolly and articulately stating the case for equality in the armed services.

At one point, he had a one-on-one meeting with a senator who asked him, "Why can't you keep your private life private?" As Tracy recalls it: "I said, 'Sir, you can't keep your private life private. Nobody does. You're wearing a wedding ring on your hand, and you have a picture of your wife behind your desk here, and don't tell me you've never cared for somebody so much or had such a great weekend with someone that you came into the office here and talked about them on Monday. Nobody keeps their private life private. What you're asking me to do is consistently, consciously lie, not just not put the picture on my desk, but to consciously and consistently lie to you about who I care about and who I choose to spend my life with. That's what you're asking me to do.'"

Tracy is clearly of two minds about the frequency with which he is described as an "all-American boy." He knows that image is a powerful asset to him as a spokesman. On the other hand: "A Navy admiral I debated once told me, 'You're OK, you can serve your country, but not these others.' Well, I'm tired of this, because I don't think we should set standards that say gay people have to be all-American in order to serve their country. I just consider myself an everyday, ordinary American who wants to serve his country."

To his parents, of course, he is much more than that. His mother, reconciled to the honesty that ended his stint with the Flying Tigers, feels Tracy "has made a difference—he hasn't just thrown his career away."

Her deepest regret is that her son had to go through a period of torment, alone, before coming to terms with his sexual orientation—and that some of his anguish stemmed from fear that his parents would be hurt.

"We *do* hurt, but because of him hurting," she says. "We don't hurt because he's gay." On July 11, 1994, Tracy's discharge came up for another hearing in Fort Meyer, Virginia. Roscoe planned once again to speak on behalf of his son, but ten days earlier, he volunteered to fly a friend from West Palm Beach to Orlando. Shortly after takeoff, the Navajo crashed, and Roscoe and his passenger were killed.

As his funeral service began, a biplane circled overhead, streaming a banner with a message from his family: "Roscoe, we love you. We'll miss you."

A saddened Tracy continued to fight his discharge through the federal court system, losing at each level, and was ultimately denied a hearing by the Supreme Court in 1998.

Meanwhile, both he and his partner, Michael Begland, had themselves become lawyers and Tracy, ironically, found himself working as a clerk with one of the courts—the United States Court of Appeals, headquartered in Richmond—that had rejected his complaint against the Navy.

About the time the Supreme Court declined to hear his case, Tracy and Michael had a commitment ceremony at Richmond's St. Thomas Episcopal Church. Conducted by the rector of St. Thomas before an overflow crowd of some two hundred people, it was followed by a gala reception at their nearby home.

What would Tracy's father have thought of the occasion?

To Roscoe, presumably—while he probably wouldn't want to talk about it—the gender of his son's life partner would be no more important than whether Michael happened to be left-handed or suffered from ingrown toenails.

The Supercop

A *Portland Oregonian* story about Tom Potter's family won an in-house award and a commendation as the "consummate story of parental acceptance." It quoted a local psychologist's blunt assessment: "Something right happened in that family."

No one can know the Potters without coming to the same conclusion. Now retired and living with his present wife, Karin Hansen, in a meticulously kept bungalow with a dramatic view of Portland's downtown skyline, much of Tom's life is centered on his four children, their mates, and his eleven grandchildren. They all live within a few miles of each other and gather at Tom and Karin's house once a month or so for a spirited clan dinner that sometimes includes Tom's ex-wife, Ginger, the mother of his children.

Tom is generally acknowledged as one of the most effective chiefs of police in Portland history, and a national authority as a community policing pioneer. As such, he won dozens of community, regional, and national awards, and gave the city a new look in law enforcement. In the words of the *Oregonian*, he "put in place a style of policing that emphasizes conversation and problem-solving in place of handcuffs and revolving jail doors." When he retired in mid-1993, the *Oregonian* wrote that in just three years Potter had "brought the bureau closer to the citizens than any chief in contemporary times." Bud Clark, the mayor who appointed him, called him "a very effective administrator" who took the bureau on "a huge leap forward."

But in a retirement interview, Potter predicted that he'd be remembered more for some other things: marching in full uniform in gay pride parades beside his fellow police officer and lesbian daughter, Katie. Testifying before the state legislature in favor of civil-rights protections for gays. Stating publicly that "some of the nicest people in this city are gays and lesbians." Whatever his other accomplishments, as he put it then, "I have no doubt that I will be remembered as 'the gay-rights chief.'"

His prediction would unfortunately come true, in full force, just a year later. In 1994, he was the Clinton administration's initial choice to head the federal community policing program, "COPS," but felt compelled to turn down the job after administration officials expressed fears that his support for gay rights might hamper his effectiveness with conservative police chiefs.

One afternoon shortly before his retirement, Tom and Katie Potter sat together in Tom's fifteenth-floor Police Bureau office, he in his blue uniform, she in jeans and blouse. Behind them, a picture window framed a panorama of blue skies, wispy clouds, and the office buildings of Portland. On one wall, a famous Norman Rockwell print underscored their mutual view of their profession. It showed a police officer and a little boy perched on adjacent soda fountain stools, beaming at each other in an obvious glow of good will.

Katie had come to her father's office so they could be filmed together for *Straight from the Heart*, a video (shortly thereafter nominated for an Academy Award) telling the stories of various families with gay children. Now both laughed as Tom told the interviewer that he had "trained Katie to be heterosexual."

"If I had an agenda for my children," he said, "it was for them to be normal heterosexuals. But Katie turned out to be a normal homosexual." He glanced at his daughter and added, "To me, she's just a great person. And I'm pleased to say, as the chief of police, she's a good cop."

Slim and graceful with brown hair and sparkling brown eyes, Katie bears a striking resemblance to her father. But their bond plainly goes beyond external similarities. Candor, warmth, humor, and an air of self-confidence seem also to run in the genes. Their fondness and respect for each other appear boundless.

Katie clearly deserves her father's "good cop" designation. Her air of friendly openness suggests a youthful innocence, but it masks a smooth blend of toughness, compassion, and sureness of manner that elicits respect from her peers and citizens alike.

As a child, Katie was passionately devoted to sports, and she eventually won a college softball scholarship. But from age five, impelled by her affection and respect for her father, she had thought about becoming a cop. Her fondest fantasy—patrolling at her father's side—never came to pass. "I had these dreams about a father-daughter team on the street in a squad car. I still think it would be neat." But long before Katie reached the academy, her father was moving up in the department and away from the street.

Growing up, despite her confident bearing, she was tormented inwardly by unwanted crushes on other girls and women. "I don't *want* to feel this," she told herself.

Alerted primarily by her tomboy nature, her father had early begun to consider the possibility that Katie might be gay. To him, it was not a daunting prospect, despite an early background some might think at odds with his accepting attitude. Raised a Southern Baptist in Mississippi until his family moved to Portland when he was ten, he had even, at the urging of his deeply religious mother, spent two years in a San Francisco seminary run by Baptists. But as a schoolboy in Portland, he sat next to black youngsters whose pains and joys seemed no different from his own. Later, he worked at various jobs with all kinds of people, including some who were gay. The relatively cramped world view of his early church upbringing was broadened into a passion for inclusiveness. So the possibility that Katie might not be a heterosexual never disturbed him.

The first thing to put him on notice, Tom says, was her devotion to jeans. "When they were little," he says, "we would dress Katie and Kim in pretty little dresses for church on Sunday. Kim would want to keep her dress on all day. But Katie would take hers off as soon as we got home and put on jeans."

Katie's path was eased by signals of her father's understanding and tolerance. She remembers an incident when she was fifteen when she, sister Kim, and Tom were going to pick up napkins for Kim's wedding. Katie froze when the subject suddenly turned to homosexuality and Kim expressed a certain distaste. But she relaxed when her father casually assured Kim that "they're just like everybody else."

Still, it would be another four years before she came out to her father. It happened over tacos at a Mexican restaurant, and Tom says he had guessed what she was planning when Katie invited him out: "It made me suspicious, because normally old Dad foots the bill for that." Unsurprised by the news, he assured her he would do everything he could to help her feel comfortable with herself or smooth the way with other family members.

Katie's siblings—Troy and Kim, both older than Katie, and younger brother Kevin—all took the news in stride, but her mother had deep religious qualms. Ginger and Tom had been divorced a few years before, and Ginger had been bitter for a time. But their mutual stake in the children spurred a renewal of good relations.

So when Tom and Katie suggested that Ginger attend a PFLAG meeting, she agreed. There, she met other parents who had had to overcome similar religious misgivings, and recovery began.

Ginger says it was relatively easy to recognize that what had changed was not Katie—she was still the same person—but rather Ginger's own thinking about her daughter. For her, the religion hurdle was far more difficult. Ultimately, she came to believe that God created Katie complete with her sexual orientation and "would not condemn what he created." Katie, she concluded, was simply who she was meant to be.

During his first campaign for mayor, Bud Clark had vowed to make Portland "a more compassionate place." To that end, in rapid succession, he named and fired three police chiefs who proved unable to move the bureau in the direction Clark envisioned. Finally, Clark settled on Potter, largely because of their shared commitment to the citizen-centered concept known as community policing. Still, Clark admits to some surprise when Potter announced his intent to wage open battle against what he viewed as the most important roots of social dysfunction and crime: racism, sexism, and homophobia.

Potter kept his vow. His hiring and promotion innovations enriched the bureau's gender and ethnic mix. Revised training programs stressed sensitivity to minorities and women. As one reporter wrote of Chief Potter, the message of equality "practically became his mantra."

Few objected to his stressing justice for women and ethnic minorities. But many Portland citizens were dismayed that he also met regularly with gay and lesbian leaders and openly recruited officers from within their community. He kept a rainbow-striped flag, a gift from the gay community, in his office.

Indeed, the crowning symbol of Potter's open management style was probably his annual appearance in full uniform in Portland's gay-pride parade. Criticized for marching in uniform, he said he did it to let the gay community know their police chief believed they deserved the rights guaranteed to all citizens.

These actions angered some officers. One, writing in the police union newspaper, berated Potter's progay stance as "gutless" and "cowardly." Potter became a leading demon and target of the state's powerful Radical Right. But he retained the support of city officials, and his opinions were paramount in the selection of his successor—Charles Moose, Portland's first African-American police chief. (Nearly ten years later, as police chief of Montgomery County, Maryland, Moose would achieve worldwide fame for his handling of a series of sniper shootings in the Washington, D.C., suburban area.)

Tom had always told Katie not to be deterred from coming out by concerns for his career. So in early 1991, when a writer for a local gay journal suggested doing a feature story about them, Katie agreed and Tom cooperated fully. As soon as the publication hit the stands—with pictures of the smiling, uniformed father-and-daughter team all across the front cover—the mainstream media swarmed over the story. A proud and openly gay police officer, openly supported by an equally proud father who was also her chief, added up to a front-page nugget.

Within the bureau, Tom says, Katie took most of the heat. "As chief, you don't have a lot of people in the organization telling you, 'Hey, I think you and your daughter are full of it.' But I don't think she realized the firestorm that would come down on *her* head."

Katie had built a network of close friends within the bureau, but others turned hostile. Wild rumors circulated that she was having sex with young girls. Her personal car was vandalized when she parked it in the police parking lot during a gay-pride parade. One officer with whom she had been on joking-around terms stopped talking to her; others made snide remarks about the gay-pride parade in her presence. She was the butt of subtle but pointed insults: the officer handing out car keys and radios to her shift, for example, would sometimes ignore her, forcing her to walk around the counter to gather her own equipment.

The harassment dwindled over the years, but Katie notes in soft tones, "I don't know if I've ever told him, but I don't think I'd still be in the bureau if it wasn't for Dad's support. He gave me the understanding and strength to keep going, assuring me that we did the right thing."

Tom, with the perspective of greater age, sees Katie as a "kind of a lightning rod" for a force that is already beginning to play itself out. In the 1960s, cops had to learn to accept blacks, and then in the 1970s, to accept women. During Tom's tenure, there was just one group it was still acceptable to hate, to call dirty names, and to discriminate against, and that was gay people. But Potter has always been optimistic that cops would eventually learn to accept them, too—and become better cops in the process. And in the decade following his retirement, the situation had indeed already changed significantly for the better. (See Chapter Ten.)

When pressed, Tom will admit he didn't wholly avoid the ugliness triggered by Katie's coming out. During the 1992 gay-pride celebration, for example, a television reporter approached him to check a rumor she had heard at an antigay press conference held earlier that day. "She looked at me, mike in hand, cameras rolling, and said, 'The rumor is that you have sex with small boys. Is that true?'" Tom was so startled at the question, all he could do was laugh. Only later, when he thought about the mean-spiritedness behind the rumor, did he become angry.

Similar nastiness followed him down to his final press conference, at which he announced his retirement. He was stepping down, he said, because he felt he had accomplished what he had set out to do, and because he wanted to do new things, such as travel and pursue his interest in archaeology. A reporter asked, "But how is your health?" It was fine, Tom answered, with the possible exception of a little high blood pressure. Later, in private, the reporter told him he had gotten a call from someone in the Police Bureau who said Potter was retiring because he had AIDS.

"Some people are so homophobic," he says, "they can't understand that anyone would support gays and lesbians simply because it's the right thing to do, or because gays and lesbians are decent and caring people entitled to their civil rights. They have to imagine, 'Well, he must be one of those himself.'"

The same Portland psychologist who said "something right" had happened in the Potter family was also quoted in the *Oregonian* as marveling at Tom's apparent unconcern about the jeopardy to his own position or the inevitable vilification of him as the father of a lesbian. To Katie, though, her father's indifference to such matters was hardly cause for surprise.

"I see how people might feel he risked everything, and I'm very proud of him," she says. "But to me it's just the way he's always been. He was just being normal."

In the closing weeks of Tom's tenure, Tom and Katie appeared together to deliver a thank-you to a PFLAG regional conference in Portland. The *Oregonian* reported the event with a banner headline spread over a three-column picture of Tom kissing Katie in front of a huge PFLAG pennant. It was the emotional highlight of the conference, as delegates stood in a prolonged ovation for their favorite father-daughter team. Some years before, as captain of the downtown police precinct, Tom had allowed the local chapter to use a large meeting room in precinct headquarters. He had also attended meetings frequently with Katie and a few times with Katie's mother, Ginger. And now the delegates cheered as he told them, "Some officers felt I was tarnishing the badge. I felt I was burnishing it."

Many of the PFLAGers who rose to applaud that day were longtime Potter family friends. They had quietly rooted for years as the Potter family survived homosexuality, divorce, and political mudslinging to carve its special niche in Portland history.

8

Family Values

Each January 1, the national news spotlight falls on the first baby to be born in the new year. In 2003, the honor went to Liana Rubin Bare, born in a suburban Washington, D.C., hospital at one minute after midnight on New Year's Day.

The usual throng of reporters, microphones, and cameras cluttered the hospital lobby. It was the traditional New Year's Day media circus—in all ways but one. And because of that one difference, as the *Washington Post* put it, "neither the media crowd . . . nor the legal system in Virginia was fully ready for this baby and its family."

The photographers asked if they could get pictures of the mother. Presumably, they had in mind Helen Rubin, who had given birth to five-pound, two-ounce Liana. But they were answered by Helen's life partner of twelve years, Joanna Bare.

"Sure—which mother would you like?" Joanna asked.

However unprepared the media might be, Liana's birth focused national attention on a matter, openly gay parenting, that by then had already become widespread, though largely unnoticed by mainstream

America. Tens of thousands of families around the country are headed by two moms or two dads.

And in many cases, at least unofficially, by two moms *and* two dads.

Danielle Silber grew up, as will Liana, with two mothers. But Danielle, now a student at Washington University in St. Louis, says she actually had "four amazing, loving parents." A gay male couple, one of whom who is her biological father, also played active roles in her rearing.

Gary Morin is another gay parent in Montgomery County, where Liana now lives and Danielle grew up. He adopted a son thirteen years ago and calls his sexual orientation a "non-issue." The reality is, he says, that gay parents "have been out there for years. We're just not covering up or using euphemisms anymore."

They nevertheless are still being harassed in many states. Helen Rubin and Joanna Bare, for example, felt compelled to move to Montgomery County from nearby northern Virginia a week before Liana's birth. Virginia courts have been hostile to lesbian mothers and state law doesn't allow second-parent adoption. So Bare—who now will have to commute to her management-consultant job in Virginia—would not have been able to share full parental rights there. The couple's lawyer said, "Quite frankly, in these matters of law, Virginia is being dragged kicking and screaming into the twentieth century—and we're in the twenty-first century."

By contrast to the state's cool attitude, Helen's father, Howard Rubin, said he viewed Liana no differently, and no less proudly, than his friends who have grandchildren view theirs.

Liana is one of an estimated ten million children living with three million gay or lesbian parents in the United States, according to Dr. Robert Needleman in his revised edition of Dr. Benjamin Spock's *Baby and Child Care.* (In other countries, the incidence may be even higher; a recent study showed that twenty percent of all gay people in Scotland are parents.) According to Dr. Needleman, "Many studies have shown that there is no difference between the well-being of children raised by heterosexual parents and those raised by gay or lesbian parents." However, he adds, there is a difference in the likelihood of sexual abuse of the children, which "is statistically less likely to happen with gay and lesbian parents." Most intrafamily sexual abuse, he writes, is committed by heterosexual males.

According to a 2003 census report, one-third of all lesbian couples and one-fifth of male couples had children living in their homes.

Any problems that Liana's parents might have faced in Virginia pale before what did happen to Steven Lofton and Roger Croteau in Florida.

When entertainer Rosie O'Donnell revealed her lesbianism to Diane Sawyer on ABC, she said her coming out was prompted by the case of Lofton and Croteau. As the mother of three adopted children of her own, O'Donnell said she thought about her own son, Parker, six, when she heard that Florida wanted to take from the two men a then nine-year-old boy who had been with them and their other children since he was nine weeks old.

It would be difficult to find more dedicated parents than Steven and Roger—"Dad" and "Rodge" to five foster children, all born HIV-positive. In 1998, the two fathers, both pediatric nurses, received the outstanding foster parents award from the Children's Home Society, a state-licensed Florida placement agency.

Their four boys and one girl have grown up thinking of themselves as brothers and sister—laughing, playing, fighting, and teasing, à la the

Cleavers themselves. They're the center of their fathers' lives. Because of the demands of caring for children with HIV, Steven gave up his job to become a full-time stay-at-home dad. He served as a parent volunteer at school and as president of the Parent Student Teacher Association. Roger, who cooks all their meals, served as PSTA vice president.

It is a child-friendly home, a comfortable place for the kids' friends to visit or have dinner. The family, often joined by the children's friends, enjoy outings at the beach or park. The men assign the children household responsibilities such as yard work, car maintenance, and cooking. They supervise the seemingly endless dosage of pills demanded by the HIV syndrome.

In 2001, however, when the oldest child, Frank, was thirteen and the youngest, Ernie, was four, the dads found themselves in court in an effort to prevent the state from removing nine-year-old Bert from the only family he had ever known. In a classic irony, the threat arose because Bert had become HIV-free: his body "sero-reverted," that is, somehow rid itself of HIV antibodies.

Hence, as a healthy, emotionally sound child, Bert was suddenly a good candidate for adoption—and Florida law banned gays from adopting. State social workers told Steven and Roger they were actively looking for another home for Bert—a happy, well-adjusted boy convinced in his own mind that he already had a home.

A federal district court held that the state did indeed have the right to tear Bert away from his family. But the court reached that conclusion in a written opinion that could not have made clearer the illogic—in this instance, the downright inhumanity—of the state law. Despite its legal holding, the opinion highlights both the cultural merit of gay parenting and the hollowness of the "family values" stance of its opponents.

The court quickly disposed of the state's argument that Steven and Roger were not heads of a "family." "[M]ere biological ties," it said, are not the essence of what constitutes a family; rather, it is "the emotional attachments that derive from the intimacy of daily association" that provide both the personal and the societal importance of family.

The court next rejected out of hand the state's contention that a trial would be needed to determine whether the requisite emotional attachments existed in this instance. There could be no question that the ties here were "quite close—as close as those between biological parents," and amounted to "a deeply loving and interdependent relationship."

So Steven and Roger can point to a conclusive legal finding that they are in fact competent, loving parents of a family unit that possesses all the qualities that make families the very underpinning of our social structure.

Nevertheless, the court ruled against Steven and Roger. Because Florida law (like that of several other states) says that gays cannot legally adopt, the court said the men have no power to prevent the state from taking the boy from his "deeply loving" family if it sees fit. In effect, it ruled that a state is perfectly free as a matter of law to ignore what the court found to be quite obvious as a matter of fact: namely, that intimacy and attachment, not biological ties, are what give a family its "importance to the individuals and to society."

O'Donnell said the case made her think about her son Parker: "My Lord, if somebody came to me now and said . . . 'We're going to take him now because you're gay,' my world would collapse."

In the late 1990's, Dad, Rodge and three of the children moved from Florida to Portland, Oregon, where the state soon placed two more boys, eight and five, in their care. But the move came under an interstate agreement that, as I write, leaves Bert subject to the Florida law that threatens to strip him from the Portland home, the school where he attends sixth grade, and the only family he has ever known.

In March of 2003, an appeals court in Atlanta took the case under consideration. Perhaps, hopefully, by the time you read this, the court of appeals will have reversed the decision—and halted the state of Florida's potentially life-shattering cruelty toward little Bert.

Every month or so, Tom Potter and his wife, Karin Hansen, brew up a huge batch of shrimp gumbo and watch it joyfully devoured by an extended family that includes eleven grandchildren of the former Portland, Oregon, chief of police. (See Chapter 7.) It's a happy clan, and typically none is happier than granddaughter MacKenzie Potter-Moen, who had turned three shortly before one sunny August Sunday afternoon when Myrna and I were privileged to share in the family fun.

"Kenzie" is a prancing child of boundless energy and curiosity whose sunny face is bathed in a seemingly permanent impish grin. She's the daughter of two police officers, Katie Potter and Pam Moen, born to Katie by artificial insemination and adopted by Pam. At the moment, Katie is again pregnant (and seven months later would provide Kenzie with a little sister, Madison Lynn) via the same process and same biological father. Although the donor is anonymous, Katie and Pam in one sense feel they know him intimately, via a lengthy, minutely-detailed agency profile of his vital statistics and personal characteristics. (He's what is known as an "identity release donor," which means that Kenzie and "Maddy," at age 18, will each have the option of meeting their father personally.)

Now, Katie and Pam are relieved to see that Kenzie is digging into the gumbo. She's been on a green-salad-and-ranch-dressing kick for the past week or so, in keeping with her penchant for falling in love with some particular dish and asking for it over and over.

Unlike her mother as a child, Kenzie shows not the slightest tendency to become a tomboy. She loves ballet, frilly dresses, fingernail polish, long hair, and what Katie calls "all the princesses in the Disney videos." To Katie and Pam, that's proof positive of the overriding importance of biology over environment as factors in personal identity.

"In our house, neither Pam nor I own one single dress," Katie says. Both have always disliked dresses and fingernail paint, and use makeup only sparingly. But Kenzie provides a stark, charming contrast to her birth mother's aversion to skirts.

"Someone said to me, 'That must be hard for you,'" Katie recalls. "I just told them it's not at all hard to encourage Kenzie to be who she is.

"So we've put her in ballet class, painted her room pink, put all her princess stuff up everywhere, and she's perfectly happy."

Sitting between Katie and Pam in a horse-drawn carriage at the head of Portland's 2002 gay-pride parade, with Tom and Karin marching alongside, Kenzie's ultrafeminine traits did not lessen her excitement at the massive cheers and applause of the lesbians and gay men who lined the parade route. Katie was the celebration's grand marshal, so honored for a dogged, year-long campaign in which she successfully lobbied city officials to extend death and disability benefits to same-sex partners of firefighters and police officers.

Shortly before Kenzie's birth, Katie left patrol duty for a part-time stint with the fire and police disability and retirement fund, where her attention was drawn to the fact that the fund allowed the benefits only to officers' legally married spouses. That left her own family, among many others, in a precarious position.

"It was glaring to me," she says, "how unfair it was to a family like mine when they retired, or something happened to them. Pam and I have a house together, with one child and another on the way. We could lose our partner and at the same time lose our home and our ability to support our children properly—all of those things that are in place as long as you're married. But of course we can't fix the problem by getting married."

Katie's argument ultimately prevailed with the mayor and council, and benefits are now available to same-sex partners of firefighters and police officers, though not to unmarried partners of heterosexual members of either department.

Kenzie calls Katie "Momma" and Pam "Mom." When she once asked if something had happened to her father, her mothers explained that there are different kinds of families, and that some have two mothers or two fathers. The explanation was reinforced shortly thereafter when Kenzie saw a television program with a family headed by only one man. And at what Katie and Pam call their "baby group"—seven lesbian couples with children who meet regularly—Kenzie now sees several families identical in makeup to her own.

Kenzie's obvious femininity seems to confirm the observation in a late edition of the Dr. Spock book on baby and child care that children of gay families are no more likely to be gay than those raised in traditional families. Moreover, it adds, "these children are often more tolerant of different sexual orientations and more sensitive to minority status."

The American Academy of Pediatrics issued a strong statement in support of gay parenting in 2002. It cited what it termed a considerable body of professional literature that suggests children with gay parents are just as well off in all ways—in "health, adjustment, and development"—as children whose parents are heterosexual. And it explicitly endorsed second-parent adoption as important to the "financial, psychological, and legal security that results from having both parents legally recognized."

"Every study I've read to date indicates that children of homosexual parents have no developmental hindrances or disadvantages as compared to children of heterosexual parents," says Dr. Pepper Schwartz, professor of sociology at the University of Washington in Seattle and author of *The Gender of Sexuality*. In fact, the professor found that children raised by lesbian mothers often show even higher levels than average of such qualities as maturity, independence, tolerance, and verbal ability, and she attributes that to the very fact that they've had to learn how to deal with the problems they face stemming from lingering social stigma.

Gay and lesbian community centers now offer a range of family activities. Every summer, more than four hundred gay-parented families gather in Provincetown, Massachusetts, for a Family Week celebration sponsored by COLAGE, which stands for Children of Lesbians and Gays Everywhere. Sample activities: sing-alongs, play groups, crafts, story time, "family carnival," sand-castle building, and workshops on such topics as "spirituality/religion," "dealing with school and friends" and "sharing stories about our families."

The families have their own glossy bimonthly magazine, *And Baby*, launched in 2001; a recent issue carried articles entitled "Dollars and Sense," "In Good Care," "Outings," and "Getting Schooled." A radio show, "Tuned In to Modern Parenting," airing in more than fifty cities, is specially geared to gay parents and their families.

Some churches are beginning to add their support. The Iowa Conference of the United Church of Christ, for example, has held weekend retreats, labeled the Rainbow Family Camp, for gay families.

The path to adulthood is almost certain to present special problems for kids like Liana, Bert Lofton-Croteau, Parker O'Donnell, and Kenzie Potter-Moen. Like their same-sex parents, they probably will face their own "coming-out" questions about whom to tell about the nature of their families. Chances are they'll have to learn to deal with a certain amount of teasing and discrimination from their peers at school. But it's also likely that they will emerge stronger persons for dealing with those tests.

And one day, presumably, the perceived differences between traditional and gay families will fade. The need for separate support services geared exclusively to gay families will disappear. And the difficulties facing their children will become the same as those of all their contemporaries.

9

The Spiritual Dimension: Four Families Confront Their Churches

On October 23, 1999, Jerry Falwell apologized on national television—while reiterating his conviction that homosexuality is a sin—for having misrepresented the gay community in some of his public statements. The apology followed an extraordinary breakfast attended by two hundred Falwell followers and two hundred members of a "reconciliation pilgrimage" headed by openly gay Reverend Mel White, a onetime Falwell ghostwriter and colleague.

White is now executive director of Soulforce, an interfaith movement committed to ending what it calls "spiritual violence perpetuated by religious policies and teachings" against gays. The Soulforce board is chaired by Jimmy Creech, who as a Methodist minister won national awards from two lay groups before being defrocked by his denomination in late 1999 for blessing gay unions.

White and Creech are among the growing number of religious leaders who view organized religion's condemnation of gays as a massive moral rationalization—a cover-up for a deeply rooted, irrational cultural prejudice.

Paradoxically, churches thereby have historically shunned a cause—the gay quest for equality and openness—that in its most basic respects is genuinely spiritual. For it arises out of millions of individual decisions that acceptance of their God-given natures is part of a quest for wholeness, for actualization of their highest potential.

A few relatively small denominations have acknowledged this commonality between their institutional aims and those of the gay movement. Ordination of openly gay and lesbian ministers or rabbis has been approved by the United Church of Christ, the Unitarian-Universalist Association, and Reform Judaism. For the most part, however, mainline nonfundamentalist churches have been torn for decades by conflict between their conservative and progressive factions over these issues. Proposals to soften their traditionally negative positions have been introduced with regularity. But the measures track a discouragingly predictable path—overwhelmingly favorable recommendation by denominational study groups followed by overwhelming rejection by the denominations at large.

Representatives of the conservative arms of mainstream denominations—Catholic, Protestant, and Jewish alike—conscientiously reiterate the illogical rationalizations that serve as the supposed moral underpinning of much of society's pervasive antigay rhetoric.

They proclaim that they act in the name of a loving God, while in effect facilitating the cruel oppression of a class of their fellow citizens. They purport to uphold "family values," but support attitudes that among other things turn parents against offspring, deprive abandoned children of loving substitute families (see Chapter 8), and generally encourage deceit and fear. They decry promiscuity among gays, but pay little attention to similar behavior among heterosexuals, while denying gay couples the formality of the non-gay world's most effective induce-ment to monogamy—legal sanction of their unions.

The fissure between gay-friendly and antigay factions has ruptured virtually every mainline church. Often, the split focuses on proposals to ordain openly gay ministers. Presbyterian, Episcopalian, and Lutheran study groups, by wide margins, have all urged such a policy. But their proposals typically meet the same fate as that of one United Methodist study committee that, by a vote of seventeen to four, recommended rev-ocation of the church position that homosexuality is "incompatible with Christian teachings"—only to see its careful work undone by a three-to-one margin at the Methodist General Conference.

This common pattern demonstrates a couple of truths. The study groups' overwhelmingly gay-friendly recommendations plainly indicate that it is almost impossible for those who look closely at the actual facts to support their churches' traditional negativism. But just as plainly, most rank-and-file churchgoers are unwilling to undertake that neces-sary step of self-education.

In all of these denominations, parents of gay children are among those working to make their churches more open and accepting places. PFLAG's ranks, for example, include numerous ministers, priests, and rabbis; seven clergymen, four of them bishops, were among its early hon-orary directors. To all of these, lay and clergy alike, the connections among religion, spirituality, and gay civil rights are plain.

Consider the experiences of four families.

Wayne and Sandra Schow

Retired Methodist bishop Melvin J. Wheatley, Jr., has said, "We were not wise enough to pray for gay children, but now we are smart enough to thank God for sending those gay children to us." At first blush, it's hard to believe that deeply religious Mormons Wayne and Sandra Schow of Pocatello, Idaho, would be among the ranks of the grateful.

Their son, Bradley, was the first person in his state to die of AIDS.

Preston, Idaho, is a farm town of 3,500 souls in picturesque Cache Valley, in the southeast corner of the state. It was there, alongside the Bear River and ringed by a majestic stretch of the Rocky Mountains, that Wayne and Sandra Schow met and became high school sweethearts. Three miles down Highway 91 is a massive road sign announcing the site in foot-high letters as the "Birthplace of Ezra Taft Benson." Nationally, Benson was best known as one of President Eisenhower's cabinet members. But here, less than two hours north of the Mormon Tabernacle in Salt Lake City, he is revered for his decade-long incumbency, ending with his death in 1994, as first president (the "Prophet, seer, and revelator") of the approximately twelve-million-strong Church of Latter-Day Saints.

Wayne says that Mormonism was a force "whose outlook and values and political power dominated all aspects" of his and Sandra's early lives. Their families had been Mormon for generations. Virtually all of their relatives lived in either Idaho or Utah, where cultural, commercial, and media influences radiated wholly from Salt Lake City. Shortly after high school graduation, Wayne spent thirty months in Denmark on a church proselytizing mission.

Wayne and Sandra were married in the church's Logan Temple shortly after he returned from Denmark. Wayne undertook a scholarly career, which ultimately led to the chairmanship of the English Department at Idaho State University in Pocatello, less than an hour's drive north of Preston. There, they raised four sons in the same rigorous

Mormon tradition; three of the boys ultimately fulfilled foreign prosely-tizing missions.

To be raised as a Mormon, Wayne has written, "is to be subjected to a formidable process of indoctrination; Sunday School, Primary, Aaronic Preisthood activity, daily seminary instruction during high school years, a variety of special worship services, and youth confer-ences." In this way, he says, the faith "absorbs one's time and attention"; it claims to have "answers for virtually all of life's great questions." And the inevitable answer regarding homosexuality is, "No!"

Brad, oldest of the four Schow sons, was born in 1958. He was a handsome, sandy-haired, gregarious boy with the broad-shouldered, slim-hipped, muscular build that suggested the strong swimmer he was. He played the piano well; he was a member of the church choir and during high school sang with a popular small group known as the Ambassadors. His broad circle of friends, drawn largely from his daily seminary classes, included both boys and girls, and a number of high school athletes. Sandra says he loved to have fun.

To his parents, though, it was Brad's wide-ranging intellectual inter-ests and philosophical bent that were most striking about him. He had what Wayne calls a "sticky mind," with a sharp questioning streak and "a good BS detector." "It was wonderful how often I would lay on him some platitude and he would challenge me on it and force me to back up."

Brad had been aware since grade school that he was sexually attracted to males. He had a series of unspoken crushes on the wrestlers and football players who were his closest high school friends. He was beset, as his father later wrote, by "an inclination that was, in the con-text of his world, unthinkable."

Just before his twentieth birthday he told his parents he was gay.

In retrospect, they say, they were woefully unprepared for the announcement.

"He knew, I am sure," Wayne says, "that we still did love him. But we could not say, 'Listen to the voice within you, Brad, and follow it. Go with our blessing: find and nourish who you really are.' We could not say it . . . how could we give him license to 'become' something we had been taught to abominate?"

Wayne was convinced that homosexuality stemmed from bad parenting or bad family relationships, and couldn't believe that applied to the Schows. He thought homosexuality had no place in any decent person's life—that "it was a choice, a bad choice, and perverse." So his initial reaction was that "this simply was not a possibility in our family"—that Brad was temporarily confused. He told his son to be patient, that the first time Brad experienced sex with a woman, "you're going to feel a lot different about this."

For her part, Sandra was initially overwhelmed by guilt. "Everything I read said it was my fault." And she knew that at church, she'd be told all she had to do was pray about it, "or that I needed to change something about myself."

Because he had not yet engaged in homosexual behavior, Brad was qualified to participate in the church's mission program. But breaking with family tradition, he concluded he could not do so without denying his identity. Shortly thereafter, in 1980, he made another fateful decision. He had found a gay companion who was moving to Los Angeles to enroll in a graduate program at UCLA; Brad decided to go with him.

Brad settled in West Hollywood, a virtually all-gay enclave, where he participated in the easygoing lifestyle typical of gay communities prior to the mid-1980s. Wayne visited him there only briefly, but it was long enough for him to absorb his first important lesson from having a gay child. "Meeting his friends was a door opener," he says. "I found they were normal people. They were healthy human beings. They did interesting things."

Mostly through Brad, Wayne came to know homosexual people back home, including a number of his own students and some of his colleagues. Recalling that, his eyebrows lift in tribute to the pleasant surprise it brought: "They turned out to be among the brightest and most sensitive people I knew."

In 1983, Brad split up with his companion. He began to feel that the hedonistic culture of West Hollywood was incompatible with what he needed to do. As Wayne now analyzes it, Brad had started to realize that "underlying the extremes of gay life in West Hollywood was a deep-seated nihilism . . . an attempt to cover despair."

Brad entered a program at Utah State University in Logan, just south of Preston. He felt his roots were there, in the mountain area he loved. But at the same time, he felt he was an outsider, cut off from the church, whose influence was pervasive in Logan, and unable like his classmates to look forward to having his own family. ("He loved children. He really wanted a family," Sandra says.)

But he was excited about his participation in Utah State's nationally reputed program in landscape architecture, and he thought he could put up with the hostile church-dominated environment long enough to get his degree. He persevered, toiling overtime to master the program's math requirements, where he had always had difficulty. He lived in a dormitory, and during his second year was a resident assistant.

So what happened in 1985, after what his father calls "his almost monkish retreat to northern Utah," was a cruel irony.

When he came to Pocatello that summer to help build a new family home, Brad was plainly ill. The AIDS virus, unknown when he moved to Los Angeles but apparently incubating in his blood since his time there, had begun its deadly work. He never returned to Logan, and instead spent the remaining year and a half of his life in the Pocatello home. It was a period of pain, struggle, grief, and frustration for both Brad and his parents—but a deeply meaningful growth experience as well.

Within a few weeks of his return that summer, he was hospitalized with a burst appendix, and again shortly thereafter with a postoperative infection. Blood tests indicated that he was HIV-positive. "A nurse took me out in the hallway and said, 'It's going to be a long, hard, slow death. You'd better get counseling,'" Sandra remembers.

They did not get counseling, and they told only a very few of their closest friends what was happening. "We were all in the closet," Wayne says. "We were trying to explain why our son was home, why he wasn't looking too well."

Silence was especially difficult for Sandra. At the time, she says, she felt she was going to burst open. In two instances, the pressure she felt led her to confide in friends. But, "They just couldn't handle it, and more or less dropped me."

A few months after his first hospitalization, Brad developed pneumocystis pneumonia. He said he didn't want to be hospitalized again, but his parents called an ambulance anyway when it was plain he was near death. Earlier, he had made clear he did not want to be kept alive by mechanical means, but Wayne and Sandra, unable to let him go, gave permission to put him on a respirator. And it seemed that Brad was not ready to let go, either. "Later we learned that without Brad's cooperation, the breathing tube could not have been efficiently inserted in the perilously short time left," Wayne says.

Brad survived, and even began to regain some weight. The Schows hoped for a medical breakthrough that would commute Brad's death sentence, but within another six months, his condition began to worsen rapidly. His muscles, nerves, and organs began to fail, and soon, even walking became intolerably painful. Brain lesions began to affect Brad's memory and eyesight. But his mind remained essentially clear, and he seemed to vacillate between wanting to die and wanting to live. He considered suicide, but decided to face whatever came.

His last months were filled with philosophical discussions with his parents. He never gave up his arduous search for faith. But in the end, Wayne says, "However much solace traditional faith might have provided, he went as an agnostic to face whatever lies beyond."

Wayne says that sharing Brad's ordeal "enlarged our awareness of the human condition. . . . We learned so much from the courageous, independent, and self-reliant way he faced his illness and his life. We are grateful to him; we are proud of him. He was such a fine young man.

"At this point, we can say we feel blessed to have had a son who was homosexual. It has taught me more about love. It has pushed me harder to broaden my philosophy. It has made me aware of the complexity and ultimately the beauty of diversity in God's creation more than anything I have otherwise experienced.

"It was an enormously rewarding experience to have had him in my life."

For Sandra, the experience enhanced a process of personal growth that led her to declare her independence from the church at about the time of Brad's death.

"I'm sure a lot of people think I just kind of flipped out when Brad died, but that's not the case." Rather, she says, leaving the church was the result of a decades-long progression toward gaining her own sense of identity and self-confidence. Her serious questioning (a quest that Wayne says has helped him become something of a feminist) had begun even before Brad's disclosure of gayness. But the months culminating in Brad's death solidified her resolve.

"His example of trying to be who he was, at great odds, led me to decide I had to be authentic too," she says. "I had to learn not to live my life in fear. Fear of some kind of reprimand. Fear of some kind of judgment against me that would be made by friends, people within the church, or my family. I had to face the kind of games I had been playing in relinquishing my power to someone else to tell me what I ought to be doing."

One of the first things she did for herself was to refrain from attending her own son's wedding because of church regulations that Sandra was no longer willing to heed. Like his parents before him, son Ted was married in the Logan Temple, where admission is restricted to those in good standing with the church. Certification is conditioned upon successful current completion of a two-stage "worthiness inter-view" with church officials, and Sandra decided that she could no longer submit a decision on her worthiness to others. Her family, including Ted, understood.

The Schows are convinced that the homophobia to which theirs and other churches contribute robbed their son of a happier, more ful-filling life. They see antigay attitudes—which lower gays' self-esteem, deprive their relationships of the cement of social sanction, and drive them to hedonism—as responsible for much of the promiscuity that exists in segments of the gay community and might have contributed to Brad's death.

"I wish I had [those] years to live over," Wayne says. "I would be able to do a lot better job of being a father to the son I loved so much . . . I moved as fast as I could according to the bad information I had . . . I could do a better job now."

Sandra echoes her husband:

"Brad's story could have been so different . . . if we could have had our heads out of the sand."

Carol and Ron Blakley

The Blakleys of Caldwell, Idaho, are one of countless families throughout the country who are actively encouraging their churches to live up to their own ideals of love and tolerance. But because their denomination is a relatively small one, their personal impact is perhaps more direct and apparent than that of most of their PFLAG counterparts in larger churches.

Carol has been honored by the *Boise Idaho-Statesman* as one of her region's "distinguished citizens." She organized her county mental health association and served on its board for twenty years, performed in local musical and theater productions, presided over a two-state region of the Christian Women's Fellowship, promoted the College of Idaho Fine Arts Series, organized a local community concert series, and did counseling at junior high and high school summer conferences. She also sat on her church's highest national administrative body, cared for AIDS hospice patients, chaired her county's first Art Auction and Ball, supported the gay community's Metropolitan Community Church in Boise, held leadership positions with the Girl Scouts and UNICEF, and chaired local political campaigns.

Meanwhile, she somehow found time to raise four children and work as business manager for her husband Ron's company, Blakley Engineers.

One of the Blakleys' four children, Ronee, is a successful actress. She was nominated for an Oscar as best supporting actress for her performance in *Nashville* (for which she also wrote several songs). But much of the drama in the lives of Carol and Ron has arisen from the more prosaic fact that another of their children, Stephen, was gay. That set their deep spirituality on a collision course with organized religion's pervasive hostility to homosexuality.

Carol and Ron belong to the Christian Church (Disciples of Christ), an indigenous North American denomination of approximately a million souls in the United States and Canada. Carol has been active at all levels of church affairs, and served on the denomination's General Board for eight years.

In rural Idaho, open proponents of gay rights were probably rarer than citrus trees when Steve, then twenty-one, came out to his parents in a moving letter in 1972. So while Carol and Ron fully supported Steve, they considered his sexual orientation strictly a family matter for some years. Then, in late 1976, one of the church's top officials visited Caldwell, and Carol determined to take advantage of his presence. She showed him Steve's letter, and before he left Caldwell, she had enlisted his support for a proposal to ordain openly gay ministers. As a result, a recommendation to that effect was endorsed by the 480-member General Board and presented to the church's 1977 General Assembly in Kansas City.

There, it met the usual fate of such measures: the church body as a whole rejected it. Not satisfied, antigay forces at the convention proposed a resolution condemning "the homosexual lifestyle." In response, Carol rose on the floor, clutching Steve's five-year-old letter. Shakily at first, but with increasing confidence and passion, she read it to her fellow delegates.

His revelation began by addressing several myths:

"I am a homosexual. I am not sick, nor deviate, nor mentally ill. My sexuality simply expresses itself in attraction for other men rather than women. Neither is it unnatural. I am not attracted to children, nor pain, nor heterosexual men. For me it is completely natural and right and good.

If your morality would condemn me, first consider these things: I did not choose to be homosexual, but I found myself one and have accepted it, happily, as an integral part of my personality; the morality that could condemn me for something over which I have no control must itself be without humaneness, akin to the consciousness which gassed Jews and massacred Indians; homosexuals in this country and others have for centuries been forced to lead secretive lives, in constant fear that their careers would be destroyed and the relationships with their loved ones cut off by hate and disgust.

I refuse to hate myself and I refuse to allow anyone who wishes to have continued personal contact with me to hate this essential part of my self either. I also refuse to live in the half-world of gay ghettoes, where furtive sexual liaisons pass for love and self-revulsion and secretiveness are the prevailing mode.

I do not live a life surrounded only by gay men. All my friends, both in Idaho and here, have for a long time accepted this facet of my personality without reservation, knowing that

I was a whole being not divisible into acceptable and unacceptable parts. My two beautiful sisters have shown me only warmth and love and remarkable understanding, as I hope my brother will when he is old enough to comprehend the implications of the oppressive social stigma attached to my sexuality. I will not live a life of fear and shame. Too many important matters interest me for me to spend my life concerned with other peoples' unjust and inhumane moral prejudices.

It is very important that you, as parents, not feel guilty because I, your son, am a homosexual. Guilt implies fault and fault implies a misdeed, and I cannot consider myself as some mistake, to be altered if at all possible and accepted only with resignation. I must ask you to accept me fully, as a human being worthy of respect and trust and love. I am no less than any other being simply because I am a homosexual!

Finally, I hope that you can accept this part of me without reservations and regrets. . . . I believe that your capacity to love can encompass the totality of myself and that you will know that I am the very same son that you have known for twenty-one years. If I disappoint you, I am sorry, but I cannot spend my life in apology. I must look to the future and so must you. . . .

As Carol, "choked up and teary," finished reading, thousands of delegates rose in a rousing ovation that doomed the antigay resolution. And Carol herself was launched on a career of church leadership that would include three years of service on the denomination's top policy-making body, the Administrative Committee of the General Board.

"I have never felt such power," Carol says of the ovation she received that day. "I believe the Lord was there. He opened the door and dared me step through it." But she adds, as though embarrassed by this implicit admission of the depth of her spiritual feelings, "Of course I know there are those who would say it was the devil who opened the door."

Carol received waves of requests for copies of Steve's letter, and she has distributed hundreds of copies of it over the years. Meanwhile, back home, the *Boise Idaho-Statesman* got wind of what had happened in Kansas City and picked up the story. A banner headline blared, "Caldwell Family Stands by Homosexual Son." The article blew the family out of the closet.

These events led to a deeper involvement with PFLAG and the gay community in Boise, and local gay groups have since honored both Carol and Ron with service awards. Within their church, Carol's dramatic 1977 convention appearance was the catalyst for the formation of an organization called Gay and Lesbian Affirming Disciples (GLAD). In 1985, Carol was honored with the first GLAD award, and eight years later, the annual prize was named after her. The Christian Church has become somewhat warmer to its gay and lesbian worshipers, and a few of its thirty-six regions now grant individual congregations the discretion to hire openly gay ministers.

Steve Blakley, who for many years ran a Los Angeles copywriting firm, spoke wryly of his parents' activism, describing them as "in a way, eccentric." His explanation: "They truly believe that people are good and that if you are good, others will respond in kind."

Perhaps the world needs more eccentric people.

Jane Spahr

It is not uncommon, when a marriage ends because one of the partners turns out to be gay, for the breakup to be survived by friendship, affection, and even love. Perhaps the most unusual and touching of such instances is that of Jane and Jim Spahr.

When Jim and Jane were married in 1964, they added a phrase to their vows stating that each would love the other "from now until eternity." They're now divorced, and Jim has long since remarried—but that 1964 vow is as strong as ever.

After seventeen years as an ordained minister, Jane made ecclesiastical history as the first openly gay minister to be called as a pastor of a Presbyterian church. She was ultimately denied the post by order of the denomination's highest judicial commission, and her case rocked the national church body, reflecting a deep schism in the denominational soul. Through it all, she retained Jim's staunch support, and they remain close and loving friends to this day, nearly a quarter-century after their divorce.

Jim and Jane are in frequent touch with other couples torn by the revelation that one of them is gay. Jim tells them, "Janie and I just got new information, but we're keeping our vows. We will love one another forever."

Case in point: when Jim remarried, he and his bride, Jackie, asked Jane to conduct the ceremony. And ten years later, when Jim and Jackie decided to hold a re-commitment ceremony, once again it was Jane who officiated. Jim, Jackie, and Jane are a trio of close, fast friends.

That tenth-anniversary event was held in a rose garden in Petaluma, California, and was attended by some fifty friends and family members, including Jim and Jane's two sons, Chet and Jimmy, and Jackie's daughter, Rhonda. "We all cried," Jane says. "The ceremony was touching, just beautiful. It was so good to have our whole family there together.

"Our friendship—Jim, Jackie's, and mine—continues to be such a blessing. I love them so much and cherish each time we are together."

In an unusual twist even for such an unusual tale, it was Jim who first considered the possibility that Jane was a lesbian. Almost from the beginning of their marriage, he sensed "something in Janie's life that wasn't up-front every day." He silently resolved to support her, whatever might come. Jim says he was only being selfish—that if the marriage were to end, he wanted to maintain sufficient harmony to protect his own relationship with their still very young sons. But whatever his motivation, the result has been the creation of a warm and close extended family.

Jane's personal recognition of her gayness came one day in the mid-1970s at a conference addressed by a lesbian priest, Ellen Barrett, and a gay United Church of Christ minister, Bill Johnson. As she listened, she thought "My God. This is my story." She went home, burst into the house, and said, "Jim, I've got to say this out loud: I'm a lesbian." He said, "I know. I've been waiting for you to tell me."

At the time, Jimmy was nine and Chet was seven. Their parents had already talked to them about sex some two years earlier. They had never heard about homosexuality, so when told Jane was attracted to other women, they simply accepted it without judgment. ("Because our parents were open from the start, it was much easier for us to deal with," says Jimmy, now thirty-six.) Their father told them that people would say their parents were breaking up because their mother was a lesbian, but it was just as true, he said, that they were doing so because he was heterosexual and couldn't meet her needs, either.

Jane was then an assistant minister at a Presbyterian church in San

Rafael, just south of Petaluma. Ironically, one of her close friends there was Jackie, who had not yet met Jim. Over the years, the women's friendship has only deepened.

Jackie, in fact, frequently joins Jim and Jane to speak at colleges and community groups and in counseling couples who are forced to split because one or the other is gay. They are not your typical lovers' triangle. Listen to them.

Jane: "People say things like, 'If only she had the right man.' Well, I had the right man. And Jackie is a very special person. It's a relief and joy that Jim has found someone who is right for him."

Jim: "I spent fourteen years living with Janie Spahr. I know who she is, and I know I'm damned proud to have been her partner. And I'm always the father of her children. That's quite an honor."

Jackie: "I'm sometimes asked whether I don't find the situation a little strange. I say, 'Well, Janie was my pastor long before I knew Jim, Janie and I are wonderful friends, and yes, I married Jim, and we're all doing just fine, thanks.'"

Jim says of Jane and Jackie that he marvels "at their deep, warm friendship that is totally independent of me." And he adds, "The miracle is, they both are willing to keep me around."

Jane's preaching style has been described as warm, witty, outspoken, and stimulating. She walks around the sanctuary, talks to individuals in the pews, makes a lot of eye contact. Her voice is forceful and energetic, and she's funny. "Our congregation was laughing, nodding, and very much with her every moment," says Mitzi Henderson, PFLAG's fourth president and an elder in a Palo Alto Presbyterian church where Jane has been a visiting minister.

However spellbinding she is as a preacher, Jane finds her principal fulfillment in pastoral care, in bringing her bountiful compassion to those in need. It was to fill such a role that parishioners of the Downtown Presbyterian Church in Rochester, New York, issued her the call that touched off the denominational firestorm in 1991.

She was chosen by a vote of some 90 percent of the congregation's eight hundred members to become one of four pastors at the church. But ten other Presbyterian churches in the area filed a protest with denomination authorities; the ensuing litigation focused national attention on Jane and the Presbyterians.

The specific issue in Jane's case was narrow and technical. In 1978, the Presbyterian church had banned the ordination of openly gay ministers. The ruling contained an exemption for those ordained before 1978, and Jane was ordained in 1974. So while she couldn't be defrocked, her opponents argued that the 1978 ruling barred her from actually serving as a pastor.

The case pitted entrenched authority against the advocates of a more open, inclusive, and tolerant church. The size of the chasm between the factions was revealed by the votes of the denominational bodies that heard the case. The Northeast Synod Judicial Commission upheld Jane's call by a nine-to-one vote—but was then reversed by an eleven-to-one vote of the General Assembly's Permanent Judicial Commission.

The gulf between the factions was (and remains) vast. Consider the contrasting frames of reference by which the matter of Jane's sexuality was judged. First, the lawyer for the ten Rochester churches, Julius Popinga:

We need to be explicit without embarrassing each other. We're not talking about homosexual orientation, we're not talking about proclivities, tendencies. We're talking about tactile, recip-rocal, erotic, genital stimulation between or among persons of the same sex.

Now listen to Jane:

God yearns for us to be ourselves. Being true to my orientation is the most spiritual thing that ever happened to me. . . . I love Jim, but with [my partner], it's like I've come home. It's the most wonderful, peaceful, passionate relationship.

Where Popinga and his kind look and see smut, other people, such as Jane, find integrity, beauty, love—and God.

In key respects, the church's stance resembles that of the military's "don't ask, don't tell" policy regarding gay service personnel. It doesn't bar all gay and lesbian pastors, only those who are "self-avowed and unrepentant": only those, like Jane, who are honest about it. In Rochester, for example, about the time of Jane's trial, Presbyterians were quoted as saying they knew of at least five gay ministers in their denomination in their area alone.

The Presbyterian church, of course, is not alone among American denominations in this seeming hypocrisy. But the price is high. How many highly qualified ministers do churches lose because, unlike Jane, they are unwilling to serve an institution that denies their integrity? What is the cost to its own honor when such an institution engages in blatant hypocrisy? What are the lessons it teaches its congregants?

And, critically, what do such policies say to the churches' young gay members? One writer covering Jane's trial, Joan Lambert, recalled the suicide of Bobby Griffith, which appeared to be tied so closely to the antigay teachings of his Presbyterian church, and wrote:

> *Maybe Julius Popinga is right—perhaps we should be explicit when discussing this issue: We are talking about teenagers who take razors and slice open the veins of their wrists. They take pills, or use guns. They hang themselves in their bedroom for their parents to find them. We get the picture.*

If, as Jane says, her openness about her sexuality has brought her inner peace and passion, the outer turmoil it provoked was perhaps equally inevitable. Long before it was to cost her the Rochester post that seemed so tailor-made for her, it had already caused her the loss of two other jobs. A San Rafael church eased her out as assistant minister after she told the head minister she was a lesbian. She then moved to Oakland as executive director of that city's Council of Presbyterian Churches, but that job too was cut short when her sexual orientation became an issue. Jim was enraged at this, and he made certain the local media reported the matter. "The person I loved so very much, the mother of my children, was being spat on again by the organization that's supposed to be about love," he says.

Her lesbianism now a public matter, Jane, for more than a decade thereafter, ran the Ministry of Light, later known as Spectrum, a Marin County center for lesbian, gay, bisexual, and transgendered persons. She now runs a mission project called That All May Freely Service, a joint venture of a Tiburon, California church with Rochester's Downtown Presbyterian Church.

Largely because of the church's rejection of Jane, and the underlying bias it reflects, Jim and Jackie now take a dim view of organized religion. When they appeared with Jane, Jimmy, and Chet at a PFLAG workshop, Jane was the only one of the five to express a desire to retain contact with the church. Jackie told the gathering, "Forgive me folks, I don't mean to hurt anyone, but I think the church needs to die and be resurrected from the ashes. I have a spiritual place in my heart that grieves for it." Jim said he is personally "Christian through to my toes" but, "I can't go to the church, any church." Instead, he says, PFLAG provides "the safe place, the island I need to go to every now and then to recharge." And Jimmy, speaking for himself and Chet, asks, "When you look at what this is doing to our mom, do you really expect us to go and throw something in your offering cups?"

But Jane, despite its rejection of her, has never considered leaving the church. Even as a child—when she "thought God and I were pals"—she says she knew that being a Presbyterian minister was her calling. So when the Rochester liaison fell through, she simply shifted her focus. Backed privately by ardent admirers within the denomination, she became the church's first "evangelist educator," championing acceptance of lesbians and gay men within the church. She is booked for speaking engagements at least two years in advance.

"I want this church to be a safe place for people to talk about what they need to talk about," she says. "I want to help change any system that encourages people to keep secrets. Secrets kill you from the inside out.

"We have to convey that being gay or lesbian is an incredibly spiritual thing. I will not listen to any church tell us anymore that we are not spiritual people. We heard the 'yes' inside us when the culture said 'no,' and that had to do with our deep inside which is our spirituality. When you come home to yourself, you've come home to a faith that is incredible, whether you call it a higher power or whatever. I worry for the church because it can lose its heart and its soul if it does not come to know who we are."

On that score, Jane has a soulmate in Mel White, onetime best-selling ghostwriter for such stalwarts of the religious Right as Jerry Falwell, Pat Robertson, Billy Graham, and Oliver North. White, an ordained minister, lost favor with his colleagues after coming out in 1984. Ten years later, he wrote *Stranger at the Gate*, a highly publicized book of his experiences. His ex-wife, Lyla, wrote a moving foreword to the book in which she made clear that she has never doubted their mutual love. (Like the Spahrs, the Whites remain close and share family holidays with their two sons and granddaughter.)

White says the reason he is now shunned by Falwell, Robertson, and others is that they fear the truth. For one thing, he says, gays and lesbians are physically present "at the heart" of the nation's churches. "We lead their choirs and we play their organs and we're their deacons and board members, and we have more than our share of pastors and priests and rabbis," he told Morley Safer on *60 Minutes*.

Echoing Jane's point, White said, "The closet is a place of death for gay people. Coming out is a place of life."

Bishop Mel Wheatley

A 1982 *New Yorker* article described what "sometimes seemed like a one-man crusade" within the Methodist church. The man was Bishop Melvin J. Wheatley, Jr., and the crusade was to persuade the Methodist church to view homosexuals "not as wretched sinners, but as . . . individuals of sacred worth . . . who can be Christians without qualification."

Soon, in fact, Wheatley would actually be tried for heresy—for refusing to disapprove of gay people in general and an openly gay Methodist minister in particular.

Now retired for over a decade, Wheatley was bishop of the four-state Denver Area of the United Methodist Church. During his distinguished career, he received many kudos, including honorary degrees from two major universities and designations as Stockton, California's "Young Man of the Year," the Los Angeles Church Federation's "Clergyman of the Year," and American University's "Alumnus of the Year." He and his wife, Lucile, were pioneers in the movements against racism and sexism. In the 1940s, they even moved into the home of a Japanese-American family to preserve it for the owners when, as they knew would happen, the family was taken to a relocation camp.

And in the 1970s, Wheatley became the nation's first clergyman of distinction to speak out forcibly against organized religion's general condemnation of gay people.

His opposition to antigay church pronouncements and policies put him in the national spotlight. Shortly after being profiled by the *New Yorker*, he was in the news again when another minister and eighty-eight parishioners lodged formal charges of heresy against him. Wheatley's sins, according to their complaint: he had made progay statements and appointed an openly gay minister to a Denver church.

If those strike the reader as something less than stake-burning crimes, a subsequent committee of investigation was of similar mind. The panel not only found no basis for the charges, but acknowledged the need within the church for "continuing study, reflection, and debate" on homosexuality. Wheatley, it said, "has addressed this concern in the light of Scripture, tradition, reason, and experience in keeping with the pursuit of truth characteristic of our United Methodist heritage."

The Associated Press wire story about the event included a photograph of Wheatley receiving a congratulatory hug from his son Paul in the Los Angeles church where the hearing and ruling had taken place. Another son, Jim, a lawyer, had helped present his father's case before the panel. But a third son, John, had the largest personal stake in the case. He had been his father's principal source of revelation, and most immediate motivational force, for that one-man crusade. He was gay.

It had been more than a decade since John had come out to his parents. But, Mel says, "Lucile and I never went through the agony that most PFLAG parents went through. We knew immediately that if John was gay, the stereotypes must be false." They also knew, he says, "We wouldn't feel comfortable being anywhere John wouldn't be welcome."

The seeds of Wheatley's break with denominational orthodoxy were sown in 1978, when he and Lucile hosted a Colorado meeting of the United Methodist Council of Bishops. The agenda included a motion that the council reaffirm its support for a statement on homosexuality in the church's governing law. The statement was clear and damning: "[W]e do not condone the practice of homosexuality and consider it incompatible with Christian teaching."

Wheatley alone objected. In addition to their son John, he and Lucile had long had a number of cherished friends who were gay. To the Wheatleys, as Mel told the other bishops, the church law statement was a "pronouncement on real people, not a pronouncement on a subject without a face." So he felt compelled to violate "the protocol calling for quiescent agreeableness on the part of hosts."

Mel calls this his personal coming-out statement. He told the others that he and Lucile had found their lives "incredibly enriched by gays who were living fulfilled and fulfilling lives." He described four of them in particular, including their son John and a lifelong friend, a doctor, whom Wheatley credited with having saved his life twenty-three years earlier. "The total life of each one of the four," he said, "appears to me and to Lucile to be as close to authentic Christian living as we perceive ourselves to be."

More pointedly—"out of my own sense of integrity"—Wheatley issued an ultimatum. Any public declaration of the council's pronouncement reaffirming the negative language, he insisted, must "carry the unmistakable message that the vote that launched it was not unanimous." In subsequent months, he reiterated his position to the other bishops in letters and calls.

His colleagues ignored the warning. Perhaps, misled by Wheatley's collegial and congenial manner, they underestimated his resolve. The 1980 General Conference quadrennial "state of the church" report endorsed the antigay statement without a disclaimer of unanimity, and Wheatley went public, causing an intradenominational fissure that remains agape to this day. Newspaper accounts of his dissent reveal that he wore the button of Affirmation, the Methodist gay group, throughout the 1980 convention. His stance evoked hundreds of letters, pro and con.

But this was only a trickle compared to the gusher of mail that greeted the next Wheatley foray into controversy. That came when he appointed an openly gay minister to a Denver church, and followed it up by responding to his critics with a powerful "pastoral letter" explaining the action.

In the letter, addressed to the denomination's 1981 Rocky Mountain Conference, Wheatley defended the appointment both as a matter of church law and of morality. It included some personal perspectives that Wheatley told the clergy "may help you further understand my official response." Those "personal perspectives" form a passage that is still regularly cited and circulated by both religious and lay groups and is perhaps unsurpassed in its lyric articulation of both the logic and the soul of the progay—indeed, prohuman—message.

The passage responds to the question, "Do I believe that homosexuality is a sin?"

I am an enthusiastically heterosexual male. Is my heterosexuality a virtue, a sign of righteousness, an accomplishment or victory of some kind on my part? Of course not. I had nothing whatsoever to do with my being heterosexual. My sexual orientation is a mysterious gift of God's grace, communicated through an exceedingly complex set of chemical, biological, chromosomal, hormonal, environmental, developmental factors totally outside my control. My heterosexuality is a gift—neither a virtue nor a sin. What I do with my heterosexuality, however, is my personal, moral, and spiritual responsibility. My behavior as a heterosexual may be sinful—brutal, exploitive, selfish, promiscuous, superficial. My behavior as a heterosexual, on the other hand, may be beautiful—tender, considerate, loyal, other-centered, profound.

Precisely the same distinction between being homosexual and behaving as a homosexual applies as to heterosexuals. Homosexuality, quite like heterosexuality, is neither a virtue nor an accomplishment. Homosexual orientation is a mysterious gift of God's grace communicated through an exceedingly complex set of chemical, biological, chromosomal, hormonal, environmental, developmental factors totally outside my homosexual friends' control. Their homosexuality is a gift, neither a virtue nor a sin. What they do with their homosexuality, however, is definitely their personal, moral, and spiritual responsibility. Their behavior as homosexuals may be very sinful—brutal, exploitive, selfish, promiscuous, superficial. Their behavior as homosexuals, on the other hand, may be beautiful—tender, considerate, loyal, other-centered, profound.

With this interpretation of the mystery that must be attributed to both heterosexual and homosexual orientations, I clearly do not believe that homosexuality is a sin.

Others, of course, did so believe. By now, with his progay statements and his Denver appointment, Wheatley had aroused the denomination's right wing. The heaviest fire came from an unofficial fundamentalist church caucus known as Good News. A group of its ministers attacked Wheatley's progay views generally, and said the ministerial appointment in particular would "undermine the basic foundation for our faith and Christian ethic—the Holy Scriptures." Within weeks, that sentiment sparked the heresy charges from which Wheatley was ultimately cleared.

Despite his unequivocal exoneration, Wheatley continued to draw fire from bands of die-hard fundamentalists. Good News went on inciting letters of protest. One Colorado church filed a formal request that Wheatley be "involuntarily retired." Other congregations passed votes of censure, and at least ten showed their displeasure by reducing or eliminating their contributions to the Rocky Mountain Conference.

But plaudits also flowed. As the first high churchman to openly defend gays' equality before God, Wheatley found himself with some important interdenominational support. A national "Friends of Bishop

Wheatley" committee was formed, largely to collect money to replace the withheld congregational contributions, and the effort attracted national figures. One of the nation's leading theologians, Harvard divinity professor Harvey Cox, a Baptist, said he "signed on gladly" because he believed in Wheatley's stance. R. Marvin Stuart, Wheatley's predecessor as the Methodists' Denver-area bishop, called Wheatley "exceedingly courageous" and "the essence of integrity and compassion." Other members included the Right Reverend Paul Moore, Episcopal bishop of New York, and Dottie Lamm, wife of then Colorado governor Richard Lamm.

Wheatley now says that he and his wife Lucile find more spiritual renewal in a PFLAG meeting than they do in church. He describes PFLAG as their "primary nurture and support group," a source of renewal for their long years of professional, religious, and community leadership roles. For him, the secret of PFLAG's successful support function, what he calls its "rap groups," can be found in Martin Buber's theological classic, *I and Thou*.

The heart of the Buber theology is what he termed the "I-Thou" concept. Social problems arise, he said, when one person relates to another not as a person, an entity sacred in the sight of God (a "Thou"), but as a thing (an "It"), a vehicle for the accomplishment of some selfish end. Most human relationships are "I-It" affairs. But when there is a true meeting of two persons, of "I" and "Thou," the spirit of creativity, of life enhancement, is present.

As Mel explains, "In so many of the meetings we all participate in, there is no true 'meeting' of the people who are there. Everybody speaks in a guarded way, with a low element of risk, which means a low element of trust." In other words, people are engaging in "I-It" dialogue. But not so, Wheatley says, at the rap groups. "After participating in PFLAG for a while, it began to dawn on us that we were never in a meeting where people didn't risk saying more about themselves than they ever had before."

He points out that when people at PFLAG meetings talk about the feelings engendered by knowing they have a gay child—it may merely be the sentence, "I have a gay child"—they often are saying the words for the first time. That's trust—revealing a never-before-disclosed aspect of the real you. It means you are trusting others to respond in kind and to treat your disclosure with care and consideration. At PFLAG they usually do just that. In part it happens because trust begets trust. But it also happens because at least some of the others have experienced what you're going through, and still others have parents who have or soon will be. So your words are almost certain to touch others in some meaningful place of their own. As Wheatley puts it: "Everyone there is at a degree of risk and is participating on the basis of trust. It's the 'I-Thou' factor at work.

"It produces a level of energy, of love and friendship, that reaches dimensions other groups just don't reach."

10

Public Figures and Their Gay Relatives

If you're the parent of a gay child, you're in good company.

"We are everywhere" is a slogan of the gay community, and it reflects a significant demographic truth. Sexual orientation is wholly independent of race, class, nationality, social standing, education, or religious or political ideology. As nearly as can be determined, homosexuality has occurred in roughly the same proportion in all societies, and at all levels, throughout history.

So it is hardly surprising that families of the famous are no more immune to gayness than any other. Families with gay members include leading figures in politics, entertainment, business, and the arts. For a variety of personal and professional reasons most of them remain in the closet. But it is perhaps a sign of growing social maturity that in recent years, a number of public figures have spoken out in support of gay children and other family members. They include—though in careful, politically guarded terms—the man who as I write occupies the nation's second highest elective office, Vice President Dick Cheney.

Among them, also, have been two of the world's best-selling

novelists, Stephen King and Anne Rice; two distinguished long-serving former senators, Claiborne Pell and Barry Goldwater; *Today Show* movie critic Gene Shalit; megastars Barbra Streisand and Cher; Robert MacNeil, a former lion of broadcast journalism, now a popular novelist; Robert Mosbacher, a secretary of commerce in the first Bush administration; Rep. Lynn Woolsey (D-CA), a six-term congresswoman; legendary theater impresario Joseph Papp, and a leading federal judge, Wallace Toshima.

In addition, as we shall see, numerous celebrities are outspoken in support of their gay siblings, cousins, and other close relatives.

Vice President Dick Cheney

Vice President Cheney on numerous occasions has expressed his love and support of both his daughters, one of whom, Mary, is an open lesbian who lives with a life partner and who has actively supported gay causes. And during a 2000 campaign debate, Cheney's response to a question about gay rights came as something of a bombshell to social conservatives when—unlike his Democratic debate opponent, Sen. Joseph Lieberman—he declined to rule out the propriety of gay marriage. "I think different states are likely to come to different conclusions and that's appropriate," he said. "I think we ought to do everything we can to tolerate and accommodate whatever kind of relationships people want to enter into."

Mary Cheney came out to her parents in the early 1990s, and was for some years the gay and lesbian corporate relations manager for Coors Brewing Company, where she funneled significant contributions to gay causes. She and her parents have publicly declared their love for each other, and Dick and Lynn Cheney have described her as "wonderful," "decent," and "hardworking."

But the Cheneys would seem to be confronted with a similar kind of personal/public conflict—though for them writ large on a national scale—that confounds so many parents of gay children. They love their daughter and have accepted her lesbianism, but find themselves unable to speak openly and directly about her. In an interesting way, their predicament illustrates the kinds of shackles that misguided cultural norms can impose on natural expressions of family affection.

During the campaign, Lynn Cheney declared the topic off-limits. On a network talk show, she declared that she was "simply . . . not going to talk about" either of her daughters' personal lives, including that of married heterosexual daughter Liz. But of course, the personal lives of politicians' avowedly heterosexual adult children—think, for example, of John and Caroline Kennedy, Trish and Julie Nixon, Amy Carter, Patti Davis, Ronald Reagan, Jr., and Chelsea Clinton, among many, many others—had never until that moment been off limits. (Nor, understandably, did Mrs. Cheney's pronouncement restrain her in other interviews from waxing ecstatic over her two granddaughters, children of her heterosexual daughter, Liz.)

And for her part, Mary apparently loves her father enough to have allowed herself to become something of a nonperson during the 2000 presidential campaign. About her only public comment during the campaign was a remark quoted in Time magazine: "I love my father. I don't want to be a distraction."

The flap that developed over Cheney's comments about gay marriage highlights the Cheneys' family dilemma. It was fear of just such responses that led Dick Cheney to forgo a presidential run in 1996, according to the respected investigative reporter Bob Woodward. Cheney's own personal lack of bias had earlier been demonstrated when, as secretary of defense in the first Bush administration, he strongly supported Pentagon spokesman Pete Williams (now an ABC newscaster) after Williams was publicly "outed" as gay.

Stephen King

His editor calls Stephen King "the rock star of writers." The *New York Times* calls him the world's most successful living author and one of the most prolific. His Maine home is a popular tourist quarry. The Internet swarms with websites planted by his fans.

A major 1999 news story was King's near-death encounter, while on his daily four-mile walk, with a minivan that bounced him off its windshield, collapsing a lung, chipping his spine, and fracturing a hip, leg, and four ribs. Five weeks later, he was writing again, from a wheelchair. He can't imagine life without writing.

The addiction appears to run throughout nearly his entire family. His wife Tabitha has herself published several novels, and their two sons, Joe and Owen, are both writers.

The only nonwriter in the family is daughter Naomi, an openly lesbian Unitarian-Universalist minister. "I tell her, and I think it's true, that Unitarianism is God for people who don't believe in God, and she just laughs," King told an interviewer.

Whatever her father's jesting, Naomi's life partner is in fact an eminent theologian and author. And if writing is Stephen King's addiction, his family provides his greatest pleasure. So it was that just a year after his accident, still in a wheelchair, he and Tabitha financed a lavish commitment ceremony attended by hundreds at Nashville's Opryland Hotel during the Unitarian-Universalist Association's 2000 meeting in that city.

Anne Rice

To Christopher Rice, growing up gay in New Orleans might have been a lot less daunting if he had bothered to read some of his mother's best-selling vampire thrillers, many of which are awash with homoerotic themes. But he didn't. So as what he describes as "the class fag"— because "I did plays and I was a little pretty boy and I was thin and wispy"—he put up with some typical high school harassment without the benefit of any direct home support.

He didn't come out to his parents until after graduation, when the family was on a trip to Italy. And he did it then only because he was anxious to get home to see his boyfriend and wanted to cut the trip short. His parents took the news gracefully, but his also-famous father, the since-deceased poet and painter Stan Rice, assured him that was still no excuse for going home early.

Christopher is now a writer in his own right, having published his first novel, *A Density of Souls*, at the age of twenty two in 2000. The story's main focus—you guessed it!—is a slight, gay New Orleans high schooler who is a member of the drama club and is teased as a sissy. After a twenty two-city book tour, Chris became something of a hero to young gay males around the country and immediately became a popular speaker at gay youth groups. His second book, *The Snow Garden*, came out two years later.

Anne Rice says she has always had a huge gay readership and some of her best reviews have been in gay publications. Nevertheless, she had no idea her own son was gay and she was totally shocked by the revelation. But her only concern, she says, was that Chris would face obstacles and prejudices: "I did not love him one drop less."

Cher

When Chastity Bono decided at seventeen to come out to her parents—
the onetime celebrated singing duo of Sonny and Cher, who had
divorced when Chastity was four—she told her father first. Chastity
thought the disclosure might bring her closer to her father, and feared
the opposite reaction from her mother. As it turned out, Cher got the
news first from Sonny and she was incensed—in part because she was
the last to know.

But that wasn't Cher's only problem with the news. Chastity's
expectations about how her parents would react were right on target.

Sonny had no problem with the disclosure, although as a conservative Republican congressman he would subsequently often disturb his
daughter with what she perceived to be his frequent antigay political
positions prior to his untimely death in a skiing accident in 1998.

Cher's reaction, on the other hand, belied her public and private
persona as a free-thinking, open-minded liberal, and an actress who had
won an Academy Award for her portrayal of a lesbian (in *Silkwood*). She
felt she must have done something wrong: "If only I had been a better
mother." In retrospect, she felt precisely what "people from Ohio are
supposed to feel, not mothers who are Cher, who have lots of gay
friends." Like the average Heartlands mother, equally a victim of cultural
conditioning, she ran the gamut of surprise, guilt, fear, and pain.

But that was 1986. And if Chastity's initial fears were justified, she
can now take delight in her mother's attitude. Cher has become an icon
of the gay community. She learned about PFLAG from her makeup artist
and friend Kevyn Aucoin (see Chapter 5) and was the keynote speaker at
a national PFLAG conference (PFLAG is "something really cool to belong
to," she says). She's been the willing cover-story subject of a national gay

and lesbian magazine, a supporter of a wide range of AIDS and gay organizations, and an outspoken advocate for gay parenting and same-sex marriage. To her, it is simply "silly" to think it wrong for any two people to make a commitment to each other and to a life together. And she makes the seemingly unarguable point that a child's welfare turns on whether his or her parents are loving, not whether they are gay or straight.

In short, Cher wants to do whatever she can to help parents who react as she did on learning they have a gay child ("Oh, my God, I failed") to discover the enlightening path that it opened for her.

Barbra Streisand

As a Hollywood actor, Jason Gould's major performance was in the role of the son of a psychiatrist, played by Barbra Streisand, in *The Prince of Tides*. Ten years later, Jason wrote and directed *Inside Out*, one of five movie shorts in a feature entitled *Boys Life 3*. In the thirty-minute work, Jason himself plays the role of Aaron, a gay son of two celebrities. Because of his parents' fame, Aaron is hounded by paparazzi and outed by a scandal sheet for "marrying" a man, and the theme of the short is Aaron's struggle to establish his own identity.

Inside Out closely tracks Jason's own life. The son of Streisand and actor Elliott Gould, Jason was first outed, picture and all, by the *National Enquirer*. He says he's paid a big price for his parents' fame. But he's pleased with the support his mother has given to gay causes. He says he thinks the only problem she had with learning he was gay was her desire for grandchildren—but he hasn't necessarily ruled out that possibility.

For her part, Streisand describes Jason as "a wonderful son," bright, sensitive, caring, and a gifted actor and filmmaker: "What more could a parent ask for in their child?"

Gene Shalit

Art editor and critic Gene Shalit describes himself as, "You know, that guy with the bushy hair and mustache on NBC's *Today Show*. Most *Today Show* fans would describe him as at least as entertaining as most of the films he reviews. He has interviewed virtually every big-name movie star, as well as musicians ranging in style from Isaac Stern and Leonard Bernstein to Loretta Lynn and the Grateful Dead, and he even covered the 1990 baseball lockout for *Today*.

Earlier, writing for the *Ladies Home Journal*, he published a column on movie violence which set a record that still stands for the largest volume of letters received in the 100-year history of the magazine.

He's also the father of six children, one of whom, Dr. Peter Shalit, is gay. Peter is an internist with both a medical degree and a doctorate in genetics, the author of two books, a leading authority on the treatment of AIDS, and professor of medicine at the University of Washington in Seattle. Says Gene, "Peter is humane and intelligent, and I am crazy about him."

It has been thirty years since Peter, on vacation from Cornell, came out to his father. Gene says it would have been unnatural for him not to be concerned about Peter's personal safety. "Remember, it was 1973, not now—and now ain't too hot either." But now, he says, he rarely thinks about Peter's being gay, any more than he ponders his other children's heterosexuality: "Some of my best friends are heterosexuals."

If he has any regrets, it is that Peter and his life partner of nearly twenty years have no children. "He'd be a wonderful father," Gene says.

His six children are in constant touch with each other, "and their love for each other is the most joyous aspect of my life."

Peter remembers that when he came out, he and his father talked about whether his upbringing might have had anything to do with his orientation. But his father now says he can't imagine any connection, "any more than my daughter's upbringing resulted in her being left-handed." And he has a piece of advice for others: "Many parents lie awake at night wondering if they played a role in the sexual orientation of their child. I think they should go back to sleep."

Robert Mosbacher

Robert Mosbacher's role as supportive father of a lesbian daughter hit the news in 1991, when both he and his daughter happened to deliver commencement speeches at Southern California colleges on the same day. Dr. Diane "Dee" Mosbacher began her speech by saying: "Dad and I had breakfast this morning. We had a look at each other's speeches. He would have used mine, but he's not a lesbian. I would have used his, but I am not a Republican."

Since "Dad" was President George Herbert Walker Bush's secretary of commerce, newspapers around the country played up the quote. Asked to comment, Mosbacher issued a statement. Dee, he wrote, "is my daughter and I love her." He acknowledged that they didn't always see things the same way. But "I am proud of her for what she is, and I hope she feels that way about me."

One of the responses to the news coverage came from the first President Bush, who commended Mosbacher for supporting his daughter. The Bushes and Mosbachers are decades-old friends. Growing up in Houston, Dee had played touch football with the future president and lived across the street from one of his close friends, Jim Baker, Bush's secretary of state and chief of staff.

Dee lives in San Francisco with Nanette Gartrell, her mate of nearly thirty years and, like Dee, a psychiatrist. For several years into the early 1990s, Dee was regional medical chief for mental health in San Mateo County, south of San Francisco. Nanette was the first openly lesbian faculty member at Harvard Medical School, where she was a professor for eight years before joining the University of California medical faculty in San Francisco in 1987. Something of a renaissance woman, Dee has also produced a number of successful videos. One, entitled *Straight from the Heart*, portrayed families supportive of gay children (including several of the families featured in this book) and was nominated for an Academy Award in 1995.

Gracing a table in a corner of their living room is a picture of the two women flanking the first President Bush, with Robert at Dee's side. The handwriting at the bottom says, "To Nanette, Best Wishes, George." The photograph and its inscription mask a central irony within the Mosbacher clan. For years, it was Dee's generally leftist politics, more than her sexual orientation, that most ruffled family calm. In the 1970s, for example, her sponsorship of antiwar rallies disturbed her father more than her lesbianism did. And the Mosbachers have always warmly welcomed Nanette at family gatherings, where she's referred to as Dee's spouse.

But in 1992, problems developed when Robert left the cabinet to become Bush's national campaign manager and later its chief fund-raiser. Dee was angered, first, when Republican leaders rebuked her father for meeting with a group of gay activists, but also later at the campaign in which her father played a prominent role. (At the Republican convention that year, Pat Buchanan declared a "cultural war" with gays as the enemy and the convention floor swarmed with placards reading "Family Rights Forever/Gay Rights Never"; Barbara Bush was even persuaded to remove an AIDS-awareness ribbon she was wearing.) Dee told the *Washington Post*, "I would like my father to understand . . . I would like the Bushes to understand, that it's neither expedient nor ethical what they're doing."

But the chill thawed after the election and the Mosbacher clan soon returned to its normal state of fondness and warmth that finds no conflict between family values and gay rights.

Robert MacNeil

In a profession increasingly caught up in a tabloid mentality, the *MacNeil-Lehrer NewsHour* was a sober, articulate, intelligent holdout. Now known as *The NewsHour with Jim Lehrer* since Robert MacNeil left to devote more time to writing, the program has always been the undisputed monarch of serious broadcast journalism, unafraid to sacrifice pizzazz for depth and insight.

The command post of television's most distinguished news show in 1995 was a modest book-lined office overlooking Manhattan's West Fifty-Seventh Street. One summer day shortly before MacNeil's retirement, my wife, Myrna, and I were privileged to visit there with MacNeil and his son Ian, an award-winning theatre and movie set designer. In a few hours, MacNeil would be reviewing the major events of the day for millions of viewers, and interviewing one of the astronomers who discovered the comet whose fragments had that day struck Jupiter. But now, relaxing in shirtsleeves, the *NewsHour*'s executive editor drew attention to a book lying on his desk.

It was a copy of *The Family Heart*, PFLAGer Robb Forman Dew's stirring memoir of her son's coming out. And the MacNeils were sharing their own coming-out story.

In the rich tones that eased his way to the top ranks of broadcast journalism, MacNeil told us a story not unlike those regularly heard from PFLAG parents. He described how Ian's revelation helped him be more honest with himself in a personal life crisis. And the stern visage familiar to millions took on an unwonted cast of pride and warmth as he cited Ian's own professional triumphs.

Robin, as MacNeil is generally known, spent much of his early career in England, where Ian was born and where by 1994, at thirty-four, had become the toast of international show business. His set for the revival of *An Inspector Calls* won an Olivier, the British equivalent of a Tony, and later drew raves in a hit New York run. ("Dazzlingly original" was *Playbill* magazine's description of the set in its July 1994 lead story.)

Some months earlier, father and son had sat for a *New York Times* interview that marked the first time they had together publicly addressed Ian's gayness. Robin says that he has "no desire to be a campaigner on this issue." But he realizes his celebrity status confers special significance to a father's otherwise ordinary declaration of love and support for his son. Among other things, it has led him to be the featured speaker and honoree at a New York PFLAG event.

MacNeil first publicly declared his unequivocal love for Ian in a *New York* magazine reply to a charge leveled by AIDS activist Larry Kramer that Robin had downplayed coverage of gay issues because he was embarrassed by having a gay son. The exchange ultimately led Robin to experience something of the glow so common to PFLAGers when their support triggers spontaneous shows of affection from gay gatherings. For him, it happened at that year's convention of the National Lesbian and Gay Journalists Association, where he sat on a panel with Dan Rather, Tom Brokaw, and Judy Woodward. The four were asked when they intended to "cross the threshold" and become sensitive to gay issues.

When it came Robin's turn, he said, "I crossed the threshold years ago," and told them about Ian and the Kramer charge. He said he not only loved Ian but was very proud of him, and he told them Ian had just won the Olivier. MacNeil is warmed by the memory: "Well, it got a big cheer from these people, and I felt very good about that."

Slimmer and shorter than Robin, Ian otherwise closely resembles his father. But he speaks more softly and quickly, in a clipped British accent, as he emphasizes the importance of a public figure saying, "I love my gay son."

Still, when Ian came out at age twenty, Robin was at first anxious about the implications. "I wondered, is he going to have a happy and satisfying personal and emotional life, or will it be a risky life?" Then he came to the realization, "That's up to him. You love this kid, he's a wonderful person, he has his own life to sort out, and he'd sort it out the best way."

A prolific author of both fiction and non-fiction even while on the NewsHour, Robin has since his retirement written a memoir and several novels—including one, *Breaking News*, about the news broadcast industry. But love of the theatre is another life-long passion and remains a strong bond between father and son. Robin was an aspiring actor and playwright before turning to journalism, and before Ian was born, one of Robin's plays nearly made it to production at London's Royal Court Theater—with which both Ian and Ian's collaborator and former domestic partner, Stephen Daldry, have been associated. Now, Ian and Daldry are better known for their work in

Hollywood, where Daldry won a 2003 Academy Award nomination for directing *The Hours*, of which Ian was a set designer.

The pair came out publicly in 1994 when Daldry won a Tony as director of *An Inspector Calls*, and said in his acceptance speech that he had three separate reasons for thanking Ian: he was Daldry's closest collaborator, he designed the *Inspector* set and, "he's my lover."

Claiborne Pell

On May 21, 1993, the U.S. Senate was debating what would become the first confirmation of an openly gay person to a high federal position. At issue was President Clinton's nomination of San Francisco Supervisor Roberta Achtenberg to become an assistant secretary of the Department of Housing and Urban Development. The appointment was opposed by a bloc of Republican senators whose principal objection was Achtenberg's openness as a lesbian.

Senator Jesse Helms of North Carolina expressed outrage that Achtenberg and her companion, San Francisco judge Mary Morgan, had embraced and kissed during a San Francisco gay-pride parade. (One newspaper said he referred to the nominee as "that damn lesbian," and added that if that made him look like a bigot, so be it.) Also denouncing Achtenberg on the Senate floor were Bob Dole and Nancy Kassebaum of Kansas, Missouri's Christopher Bond, and Mississippi's Trent Lott.

Among those rising to decry the nature of these attacks was Rhode Island Democrat Claiborne Pell. One of the body's most distinguished members, Pell, then seventy-four, ranked third in seniority and chaired the powerful Committee on Foreign Relations. His forebears included five members of Congress, one of whom, George Dallas, had also been James Polk's vice president. Pell had been a member of the conference that created the United Nations, and had written and sponsored scores of important pieces of legislation. His name even became part of the national lexicon in 1980 when Congress officially named a block of higher-education subsidies "Pell grants" to recognize his role in creating them. He had been decorated by no fewer than twelve foreign countries, and received honorary degrees from forty-six colleges and universities. He served six Senate terms before retiring in 1997.

Now, he told his colleagues, he had a personal reason for supporting this nomination. His daughter Julia was a lesbian and president of the Rhode Island Alliance for Gay and Lesbian Civil Rights, and he would not want to see Julia barred from a government job because of her sexual orientation. "I believe we should strive to let simple standards of fairness and equal treatment be our guide in examining all nominees that come before us," he said. "I know I would want to see my daughter treated fairly, if she were the nominee before us today."

The nomination was approved fifty-eight to thirty-one.

Julia was thirty before she realized she was gay. She immediately told her family and had their full support from the beginning. For some years before the Achtenberg debate, Senator Pell on various occasions had publicly acknowledged Julia's lesbianism, but never before on the Senate floor.

Julia helped raise her life partner's daughter, now an adult, and says she and her partner are "just an old-fashioned happily married couple."

Joe Papp

Throughout the day of November 1, 1991, New York radio and television bulletins reported the death of a "giant of the theater, creator of Shakespeare in the Park and so much more." Lights were dimmed not only on Broadway, listeners were told—"they dimmed from Avon to Central Park."

Joe Papp's New York Shakespeare Festival had brought the Bard free to the public. His seven-theater complex known as the Public Theater had provided opportunities for new playwrights, and had sent on to Broadway such hits as *A Chorus Line* and *Hair*. He had brought to the American public such stars as Meryl Streep, George C. Scott, Colleen Dewhurst, and James Earl Jones. The *Encyclopedia Britannica* calls him a "major innovative force in U.S. theater in the second half of the twentieth century." A *New York Times* reviewer called him "arguably the . . . dominant shaper of contemporary American theater."

In launching the Shakespeare Festival, Papp worked for little pay for many years and produced and directed most of the plays himself. To him, his greatest triumph was the festival's policy of providing free performances in various locations around the city, including Central Park. Opposing the notion were such legendary city powers as Parks Commissioner Robert Moses and powerful theater critic Walter Kerr. But even they had to bow before the sheer force of Papp's passion for Shakespeare and his egalitarian vision of the Elizabethan's lusty appeal to Everyman.

But if Shakespeare was a major dynamic of Joe Papp's life, a tone of Greek tragedy hovered over his lingering death. While himself terminally ill with prostate cancer, he helped nurse his son Tony, who was dying of AIDS. Tony died first, five months before his father. "When he told me about Tony's death, he let out a high-pitched, anguished cry. I had never heard that sound come out of anyone's mouth before," said actor Kevin Kline, as reported by Papp's biographer, Helen Epstein, in *Joe Papp: An American Life*.

When Tony, at age fifteen, told his father he might be gay, Joe went through the same rites of passage that most parents experience. He later admitted that it was far more difficult to accept the gayness of his own child than of someone outside the family. At first, he simply wanted to deny it. Then he was upset. Then he blamed himself. But his love for Tony ultimately led to acceptance and an enhanced closeness in their relationship. "I've learned not only to accept his gayness but to love him for it," he told the media. He said the experience "wiped out the last vestige of prejudice" he felt toward gay people.

One of the ways Joe demonstrated support for Tony was to become a major donor to New York's Hetrick-Martin Institute. The institute conducts the Harvey Milk School and other programs that benefit gay youth; Papp was drawn by the fact that its very existence told teenagers it's OK to be gay. When he allowed his name to be announced with a major donor group there, it was the impresario's way of coming out as a parent. "I want to show my affection for my son Tony, because I love him," he said. "And I want to convey a message to other parents who don't know how to deal with a child who is gay."

Lynn Woolsey

In the fall of 2002, the Associated Press reported that the Army was considering recruiting Middle Easterners to serve as interpreters in the war on terrorism, due to the severe shortage of Arab-speaking soldiers. About the same time, the same Army was discharging seven Arabic linguists, all with good service records, because they had been discovered to be gay.

If that seems inane, don't waste time complaining to Rep. Lynn Woolsey.

In 1992, in her first run for Congress, Woolsey captured a stunning 67 percent of the vote in California's Sixth Congressional District. In Washington, her first major policy stance was her outspoken support for President Clinton's proposal to end the ban on gays in the military.

She knew she could not in good conscience avoid a major role in the fight against the ban. Twenty-five years earlier, as the human resources director of an electronics firm, she had worked to extend its antidiscrimination policy to include sexual orientation. As an eight-year member of the Petaluma, California, City Council, she had become known as a champion of civil rights. She had run for Congress on human-rights issues and felt an obligation to a constituency generally liberal on social matters.

First, though, there was a private family matter to resolve.

Five years earlier, Woolsey's stepson Michael had told her he was gay. He had also told his father and sister. But Michael still was not out to his two brothers or his other relatives. Woolsey had scary visions of Michael being outed, and of her own efforts being politically ridiculed by charges that she was in the closet about having a gay son. But she left the decision about going public to Michael.

He not only agreed to do so, but joined her in Washington to lobby for repeal of the ban. In June, she and Michael appeared together at a nationally publicized press conference. They hugged and kissed for the cameras. Mother said she hoped her son could help put a "real face" on homosexuality for lawmakers. "Our family exemplifies what family values is all about," she said. "We are accepting, supporting, and loving of each other." Of Michael, she said simply, "We are proud of him." Michael called his mother's efforts "really wonderful—she's an incredible voice for civil rights, for our family values."

Ultimately, of course, the lobbying proved fruitless: Congress adopted the "don't ask, don't tell" policy on gays in the military, an obvious step backward. Woolsey subsequently introduced an ingenious piece of legislation that would reduce each year's Department of Defense budget by the amount it had spent the prior year on training, investigating, and discharging gay service members. The bill was bottled up in committee, but it served to focus a spotlight on the immense sums wasted on such military witch hunts. (The government estimates it spends $27 million a year just for the recruiting and training costs of discharged gays.) She is also an original cosponsor of the Gay and Lesbian Youth Suicide Prevention Act, which would establish a commission on gay youth within the Department of Health and Human Services.

Lynn raised Michael from age six along with her other two sons and daughter. She was the first in the family ("I was honored," she says) to whom Michael came out. His ultimate disclosure to the entire family, she says, created a positive new family dynamic of openness.

Lynn and Michael together addressed the 1994 PFLAG convention in San Francisco. There, Lynn said of her son, "I am so proud of him. He is my friend, my ally. He's my partner in politics. And most of all, he's my son. I think everybody ought to have a Michael Woolsey in their life."

In 2003, starting her sixth term in Congress, Woolsey was chair of the Democratic Caucus Task Force on Children, a senior member of the House Committee on Education and the Workforce, and the ranking member on the House Subcommittee on Energy.

A. Wallace Tashima

For lawyers who practice in the federal courts in the Western United States, the reference work of choice is *Federal Civil Procedure Before*

Trial, coauthored by Judge A. Wallace Tashima. The two-volume work is a measure of the quality craftmanship that has graced a distinguished four-decade legal career.

As a member of the Ninth Circuit Court of Appeals, Tashima sits at a level just below that of the Supreme Court. He was appointed in 1996 after sixteen years as a federal district judge in California's Central District. Earlier, he had served as a deputy state attorney general, litigation and managing partner of the Los Angeles office of a national law firm, and a member of the state Committee of Bar Examiners. As a judge, his more than one hundred written opinions form a substantial body of law ranging over virtually every area of business, constitutional, and criminal law. He has lectured on the American legal system in such far-flung spots as Egypt, Japan, and Myanmar. In 2001, he headed an American delegation invited to China by the State Intellectual Property Office of China.

The father of two sons and a daughter, Judge Tashima describes his reaction as "not positive but not grim" when his youngest child, Jonathan, disclosed he was gay in 1989. Like many parents, he had always thought of homosexuality as being abnormal. He now accepts gayness as "within the norm," but says he is still not completely comfortable with it. Even so, the Tashimas are a close-knit family, all fully supportive of Jonathan. His mother, Kiyo, is the most demonstrative: antigay comments in her presence inevitably draw an angry rebuttal. And Judge Tashima volunteered to go public in this book out of a conviction that Jonathan "has the right to live his life, like anyone else."

Tashima's sensitivity level to the issue has also been raised by the law clerks he has employed, at least three of whom have been gay. They have helped him realize that they are "just human beings" whose sexual orientation does not affect their legal talents.

Such influence by law clerks does not stop with Judge Tashima. Although the clerks function primarily as legal researchers, they also serve as judges' sounding boards in wide-ranging discussions of social and legal issues, and write drafts (and sometimes the final versions) of court opinions. So the relatively traditional thinking of sitting judges may at times be shaped by the often more progressive perspective of their clerks.

Judge Tashima recalls in particular one of his own clerks, whose partner worked for one of Tashima's older, quite conservative colleagues. The two young men, now in successful private practice, have since adopted two children; Tashima is convinced that knowing them opened the eyes of the older judge.

Barry Goldwater

To Barry Goldwater, who died just short of his ninetieth birthday in 1998, the devil's name was Hypocrisy. His forthrightness and stubborn integrity arguably cost him the American presidency because he refused to sugarcoat his views. But his uncompromising honesty gained him the status of Conscience of the Republican Party and won him the respect and affection of the country he served for thirty-seven years in the Senate.

And in his mid-eighties, it led him to speak out fiercely on behalf of gay rights—as well it might, as a social movement founded on honesty and integrity.

Goldwater for decades was the very symbol of American conservatism. So many were surprised by his devotion to gay rights. They shouldn't have been. The stance fit snugly into the character of a super-patriot, a passionate political partisan, and an outspoken exemplar of rugged individualism.

Like so many public figures, Goldwater had relatives—he specifically mentioned a grandson and a grandniece—who are gay. But unlike so many public figures (see "Vice President Dick Cheney," above), he refused to duck discussion of the issue. As he saw it, his relatives were vulnerable to unfair treatment by society, and that made the matter of political as well as personal significance. So an issue that others find awkward and confusing was, to Goldwater, crystal clear. People should be judged on their merit—period.

"It's time America realized that there was no gay exemption in the right to 'life, liberty, and the pursuit of happiness' in the Declaration of Independence," he wrote.

Hence, when President Clinton made his ill-fated proposal to end the ban against gays in the military in 1993, Goldwater—a former fighter pilot and Air Force general—backed the commander-in-chief in a widely quoted op-ed piece. "Everyone knows that gays have served honorably in the military since at least the time of Julius Caesar. They'll still be serving long after we're all dead and buried. But most Americans should be shocked to know that while the country's economy is going down the tubes, the military has wasted a half-billion dollars over the past decade chasing down gays and running them out of the armed services."

The next year, he was just as outspoken in favor of proposed federal legislation to ban employment discrimination against gays. He cited traditional Republican party principles for the proposition that in a free-market economy, "competition and the Constitution matter—and sexual orientation shouldn't."

Locally, he lent his support to measures designed to outlaw discrimination in hiring based on sexual orientation. And in 1994, he signed on as honorary cochair (with Oregon's former governor Barbara

Roberts) of a national gay-rights campaign called Americans Against Discrimination, sponsored by the leading gay lobbying organization, and formed to support a federal antidiscrimination measure and oppose various antigay initiatives around the country.

Each year, gay Americans celebrate Coming Out Day on October 11, the anniversary of the 1987 march on Washington. (See Chapter 2.) The observance serves as a reminder not only to gay people but to their families and friends that the closet is an instrument of oppression; all are encouraged to take some step toward the goal of total personal openness. For gay people, the step can be as small as attending their first meeting of a gay organization, or as big as coming out to their parents or their colleagues. For family members and friends, it might mean displaying some symbol of support of the gay movement, such as wearing a pin (a popular choice is "I'm Straight but Not Narrow") or writing a letter to the newspaper. For Barry Goldwater in 1994, it meant praising a gay grandson, Ty Ross, at a statewide rally.

Coming Out Day was a celebration of special significance to the Arizona gay community that year. Arizona was one of nine states that had recently repelled radical Right efforts to qualify an antigay initiative for the November ballot. The Arizona opposition had been led by an organization called Arizonans for Fairness, and Barry Goldwater had been its honorary chair.

Goldwater was not able to attend the rally, but he sent a letter to be read by Ty, whose voice blended pride and affection as he read his famous grandfather's words asking for "justice, fairness, and equality for gay, lesbian, and bisexual Americans."

Goldwater hailed the victory of Arizonans for Fairness, expressing particular pleasure in the fact that its campaign had been supported by most of the state's elected officials. Then he closed on a personal note: "I am especially proud that my grandson Ty is reading this letter to you. My love for him, as for all my grandchildren, is strong, and we stand together as a diverse family in our opposition to injustice and inequality."

In the entertainment world, a complete list of celebrities with gay relatives perhaps would fill several books. But here are a few who have been reported as acknowledging their love for gay or lesbian members of their immediate or extended families:

Garth Brooks in 1993 unintentionally outed his lesbian sister, Betsy Smittle, the bass player in his band, but she has now long been comfortable with the news being public.

In 2002 the *Chicago Sun Times* reported that Ben Affleck and Cyndi Lauper had agreed to appear in a PFLAG ad campaign, Affleck with his gay male cousin, Lauper with her lesbian sister Ellen.

Brooke Shields says she was raised by her mother and two gay men she has lovingly called her "fairy godmothers."

Some of the presumably legions of others include Emma Thompson (uncle), Sigourney Weaver (brother Trajan), Roseanne Barr (sister Geraldine and brother Ben), Richard Gere (brother David), and Paul McCartney (half-sister Ruth).

11

The Unreliability of Stereotypes

Each year, as more gays leave the closet, the fallacy of conventional wisdom about homosexuality grows ever more obvious. Each year, more of the archaic stereotypes are unmasked as, well, fairy tales.

Consider three important fields—policing, professional sports, and politics—in which gay participants are increasingly defying the standard limp-wrist, drag-queen, bull-dyke images.

The Cops

Sergeant Brett Parson is a casting agent's dream of a police officer: a towering, brawny, gang-busting cop who was the youngest referee in professional hockey before joining the District of Columbia Police Department in 1992. As a star of the major narcotics unit in 2000, he was the department's Officer of the Year. A year earlier, he was named a "hero of the department" after being shot at during a wild car chase and subduing the fleeing holdup man when the escape car bounced off another vehicle and crashed into a tree. A *Washington Post* profile called him "an uncommon cop," a "friendly loudmouth" who "pulls into oncoming traffic on his way to a distress call and harangues slow-moving drivers on his cruiser's loudspeaker ('In the United States, we pull to the right for emergency vehicles!')."

Brett admits to loving the fierce action and excitement of street police work. But he's also highly intelligent, articulate and outgoing—and openly, proudly gay. So in 2001, Chief Charles H. Ramsey handed him a new assignment as head of the department's Gay and Lesbian Liaison Unit. In that capacity, Brett has managed to convert much of Washington's large gay community—citizens conditioned to see cops as potential harassers and abusers—to a more police-friendly attitude. He's obviously proud of the GLLU's accomplishments, but he's restless functioning in a relatively tame post. "I'm doing this because the chief asked me to, but I feel kind of underutilized here," he says.

He'd prefer to be making homicide and narcotics busts—"stuff I can sink my teeth into." He says the GLLU assignment makes him feel "like Sylvester Stallone cast in the role of Barney Fife [the kindly but lazy deputy on "The Andy Griffith Show"]."

At the same time, it's hard for him to hide his pride in the work of the GLLU. It's part of Chief Ramsey's focus on community policing that, like that of Tom Potter in Portland (see chapter 7), seeks to forge partnerships between his department and the communities it serves. And the unit's success is obvious. A Washington television station told of a high school junior, evicted by his parents for being gay, who seriously considered suicide until Brett personally came to his aid. The unit's work has been key to the solving of a number of high-profile crimes that include the 2001 murder of gay AOL executive Doug Small, the killing of two transgender teenagers and the beating of two gay members of a college marching band.

Brett was just seventeen when he became a referee in a minor professional hockey league. A few years later, he was a University of Maryland undergraduate when he came out to his parents, Richard and Diana Parson of Laurel, Maryland, who say their only concern was that being gay might adversely affect their only son's job prospects.

They needn't have worried.

As a gay, macho cop, Brett might seem out of the ordinary. He isn't. He is one of the best known because of his very public role as head of the GLLU. But I've talked with numerous gay police officers and they all assure me that every large city force has about the same proportion of gay male officers as the population at large. A film entitled *Gay Cops: Pride Behind the Badge*, which premiered in Washington, D.C., on March 2, 2003, featured men and women in law enforcement from all across the country.

In the past, homophobia in police departments was so fierce that gay officers literally feared for their lives if they were to be outed. Gay officers told stories of failing to get the kind of backup support that can mean the difference between life and death—and even about violently homophobic officers who some feared might be tempted to send "stray" bullets their way during hectic gunfights. At best, those who did come out, and survived, were typically subjected to insults, assaults, and the kind of demeaning treatment suffered some years ago by a New York officer who said he was handcuffed and suspended from a coatrack by his fellow officers.

About the same time as that report, however, another New York officer became the first openly gay officer to be awarded the city's police department's Medal of Valor. On September 18, 1997, Mayor Rudy Giuliani bestowed the honor on Officer Tony Crespo, who was shot in the knee and slashed with a knife while attempting to save the life of another officer.

Few openly gay cops receive the kind of attention given Crespo and Brett Parson. But they are not oddities—their sexual orientation just happens by chance to have commanded public attention. At least a score of Brett's fellow gay male officers are now open about their sexuality. Katie Potter (Chapter 7) says that even in the late 1980s, when she came out, a meeting of gay officers would draw as many as forty officers from Portland and nearby small Oregon and Washington communities, although at that time most of them were otherwise closeted. Now, type the words "gay" and "police officer" into your search engine, and you might, as I did, get some 62,000 "hits." While most continue to deal with alleged police brutality against gay victims, many others refer you to large organizations of gay officers (not only in the United States but also in Australia, Canada, and Great Britain), including information about their increasingly well-attended annual national conferences.

The Jocks

Esera Tuaolo describes himself as "just your typical gay Samoan ex–nose tackle who'd like to break into show biz."

At six feet two inches and 280 pounds, Tuaolo played professional football for nine years, including a Super Bowl appearance with Atlanta in 1998. In college at Oregon State University, he was voted top defensive lineman in the Pac-10, made honorable mention All-America, set school records for sacks and tackles, and was a second-round draft choice of the Green Bay Packers. In his first National Football League season, he made the NFL all-rookie team. He is proud to count all-time Packer quarterback great Brett Favre among his personal friends from his NFL days.

But he was miserable throughout most of his football career. The NFL, he says, is a supermacho culture: "It's a place for gladiators. And gladiators aren't supposed to be gay."

On October 29, 2001, Tuaolo came out in an interview with Bryant Gumbel on HBO's "Real Sports." He talked of depression, loneliness, and thoughts of suicide brought on by the demands of a double life. At one point, as he tried to describe the antigay nastiness that pervaded the locker rooms, his voice faltered and he fought back tears. He would force himself to laugh at the antigay jokes, he said, but "inside it would be tearing me up."

The interview prompted thousands of positive e-mails, and only a few negative, from around the world. But in a *Fresno Bee* interview, San Francisco 49er running back Garrison Hearst appeared to bear out Tuaolo's point. "I don't want any faggots on my team," Hearst said. "I don't want any faggots in this locker room."

In January 2003, Tuaolo was honored at a National Press Club press conference in Washington, D.C., when PFLAG announced a scholarship to bear his name as part of the country's first national scholarship program for gay, lesbian, bisexual, and transgender students. The massive nose tackle opened his appearance by quietly asking the audience to stand. Then he delivered a stirring a cappella rendition of the "Star Spangled Banner" in a robust falsetto-style voice that one critic has called "gorgeous" and likened to that of another big man, pop legend Aaron Neville. He has already recorded some pop albums and looks forward to a career in singing and the theater.

His remarks that day focused largely on his family, consisting of his life partner of five years, Mitchell Wherley, and their adopted two-year-old twins, Mitchell and Michelle. In his football years, he said, he would often look longingly and enviously at his teammates with their wives, children, and suburban homes. He never thought the same was possible for him, he said—"but now I have a spouse, two children, two dogs, and the picket fence in the suburbs."

He also speaks tenderly of his mother, whom he credits with saving his life. He says it was the thought of her love and support, and her sacrifices after his father died when he was ten, that kept him from acting on his thoughts of killing himself during the football years.

Tuaolo is only the third NFL player ever to come out voluntarily. (A fourth, Washington Redskin tight end Jerry Smith, was known to be gay but died of AIDS in 1987 without ever acknowledging his homosexuality.) Ten years earlier, Roy Simmons, an offensive guard for the Giants and Redskins, came out on "Donahue". The first to do so, more than thirty years ago, was David Kopay, a running back who came out shortly after retiring and wrote a book, *The David Kopay Story*, that was a 1977 *New York Times* best-seller and is now in its fifth printing. Tuaolo and Kopay recently met at a party, and Tuaolo says it was a moving, emotional experience. Reading Kopay's book in 1997 changed his life, he says.

Tuaolo conjectures that every team probably has four or five gay players but that whoever they are, they managed, like Tuaolo, to keep it tightly under wraps.

It wasn't always easy for Tuaolo. He remembers occasions, for example, when he and Mitchell would be in a grocery store and see an old Viking teammate. "Mitchell would duck into the next aisle and I'd keep going. We'd pretend we didn't know each other."

Now, there's no more pretense and Esara Tuaolo is plainly comfortable as your typical gay ex-nose tackle looking for a future in show biz.

John Levesque, columnist for the *Seattle Post-Intelligencer*, wrote that men's sport in 2003 "remains the institution where homosexuality is most feared, more than a career-ending injury, more than a demotion to the bench, more than banishment or violation of league drug policy." But Tuaolo and others make it clear that gay athletes do in fact exist in significant numbers in the NFL, which makes it hardly surprising that they are broadly present across the range of big-time sports. Greg Louganis, four-time Olympic gold medalist in diving, says he has been asked for advice about coming out from athletes in a variety of pro team sports.

Among those who have come out are two ex-major league baseball players. The story of the first ended in tragedy when Glenn Burke, a former outfielder with the Los Angeles Dodgers and Oakland A's, known for populariazing the "high five," died of AIDS, a homeless drug addict, in 1995.

By contrast, the coming out of the second, Billy Bean, a former outfielder with three major league teams, has been part of an ongoing success story. Now a Florida businessman, Bean has written a well-received book, *Going the Other Way,* and speaks regularly to groups of students, athletes and adults about the empowerment of coming out. He is said to have provided much of the inspiration for the play, "Take Me Out," which opened on Broadway in 2003 and deals with a gay baseball player's coming out.

In individual sports, the numbers of acknowledged gays is significantly greater.

In tennis, International Tennis Hall of Famer Martina Navratilova has become something of a lesbian idol, an all-time great whose personal integrity, for her, commanded clear priority over the millions of dollars in potential endorsements forsworn by her public declaration. An earlier tennis star, Billie Jean King, came out about the same time as Navratilova. And way back in the 1920s, Bill Tilden—winner of two Wimbledon and seven U.S. championships, who in 1950 would be named the greatest player of the half-century—took no pains to hide his homosexuality.

In track and field, Dr. Tom Waddell, an Army physician, placed sixth in the 1968 Olympic decathlon. He later formed the Gay Olympic Games, which have been held every four years since 1982 and in 2002 drew thousands of competitors from eighty-two countries to Sydney, Australia.

In diving, two openly gay men, David Pichler and Patrick Jeffrey, competed for the United States in the 1996 Olympics. At least two skaters are "out:" Canadian Brian Orser, a former world figure skating champion and two-time Olympic silver medalist, and Matthew Hall, also a Canadian national team figure skater. Also out are Missy Grove, a world title mountain biker said to be "the Michael Jordan" of her sport, and Bruce Hayes, a 1984 Olympic gold medalist as a member of the U.S. 800-meter freestyle relay.

Dave Pallone, a major-league umpire, was fired after coming out to the National League president, and in 1990 wrote a book, *Behind the Mask: My Double Life in Baseball*, about his experiences.

These pioneering souls clearly represent the tip of a cultural iceberg. But unlike the iceberg of nature, large sections of its huge, once-hidden mass are slowly emerging into the sunlight.

The Pols

On January 6, 1999, Tammy Baldwin made history on three different counts. At thirty-six, blonde and blue-eyed with the wholesome, energetic mien of a high school cheerleader, Baldwin became (1) the first woman ever to be sworn into the United State's Congress as a representative from Wisconsin, (2) the first acknowledged lesbian to serve in either house, and (3) the first openly gay person of either sex ever to be elected to a first term.

The Unreliability of Stereotypes

As an openly gay member of Congress, Baldwin is one of history's five openly gay persons to so serve, although the other four publicly acknowledged their orientation only after some years in the House of Representatives. The number of openly gay office holders at all levels of the political scene is now approaching two hundred fifty, according to the Gay and Lesbian Victory Fund, an organization that supports such candidates. That's a tiny proportion of the nation's half-million elected officials, but it grows each year and it speaks to the increasing tolerance on the political front. Rep. Barney Frank (D-MA), perhaps the best known of openly gay politicians, says he thinks most voters "were never really all that homophobic to start with. . . . They just thought they were supposed to be."

The political makeup of history's openly gay House members attests once again to the refusal of same-sex orientation to respect geography, demography, or political philosophy. Like Baldwin, one of the other four, Steve Gunderson, also represented a Wisconsin district but differed from her both in party affiliation and the nature of his constituency; Republican Gunderson represented a rural area dominated by dairy farms, in sharp contrast to Baldwin's traditionally liberal, largely metropolitan district centered in the state capital of Madison. (Gunderson represented his district for sixteen years and was in line to chair the House Agriculture Committee when he chose to reenter private life in 1996.) Both Frank and Gerry Studds, who retired in 1996 after serving eleven terms, are Massachusetts Democrats. But the fifth, Rep. Jim Kolbe, is an Arizona Republican.

Frank is a veteran of more than thirty years of a career that elicits raves from pundits who rate him one of the most intelligent, articulate, wily, and witty representatives in House history.

At the state level, the career of Democrat Arthur J. Feltman, a Hartford lawyer now in his fourth term in the Connecticut General Assembly, had an ironic twist—he lost his first run for the city council in 1993 when he was actually "outed" by gay leaders supporting a rival candidate. But he responded in a way that neutralized the issue and paved the way for future success, by using the media to send a strong and believable message that he was a candidate who happened to be gay, not a candidate with a narrowly gay frame of reference.

"My district is primarily working class, inner city, overwhelmingly Roman Catholic. So I spent lots of time reaching out to people whose background and perspective couldn't be more different than that of gay activism."

That message—that his sexual orientation was immaterial to his willingness to work for his constituents' causes—helped him win a council seat the next time around. As a councilman and chair of a key planning committee, he initiated a bill that gained national attention while reflecting his independence from traditionally liberal gay voters—it limited the number of social service agencies, such as homeless shelters and drug-treatment clinics, in downtown areas marked for economic development. Elected to the General Assembly in 1996, he was instrumental, as vice chair of the Judiciary Committee, in the enactment of a law granting co-parent adoption rights (see chapter 8) to gay couples. He now chairs the assembly's important Public Health Committee.

Around the country, gay candidates like Feltman are increasingly demonstrating that being open about their sexual orientation is not the barrier it once was to public office. In Maryland, for example, where Rich Madaleno in 2002 became the first openly gay candidate to win a first term in the state legislature, his life partner, Mark Hodge, often campaigned with him.

"I knocked on doors by his side," said Hodge, a thirty-five-year-old school nurse. "He was never afraid to include me in things. He was very honest about who we were from the beginning." (Campaigning finished for another four years, Madaleno and Hodge immediately set about to begin their own family by placing their names in a pool with other families for adoption.)

In 2003 the Victory Fund supported eighty openly gay officials elected to a broad range of posts. Among them were thirty-one members of state legislatures; thirty-three members of city and county governing boards, including three city council members in New York City and two in the District of Columbia; trial judges in Chicago, Illinois, and Miami, Florida; the district attorney of San Diego, California; the Travis County sheriff in Austin, Texas; and the mayors of such widespread towns as Atlanta (Georgia), Tempe (Arizona), and Plattsburgh (New York).

There is of course no reason why a candidate's sexual orientation should have any bearing on a voter's judgment. But the Republican party base continues to contain an influential hard-core antigay faction to whom competence sometimes seems irrelevant. The experience of Steve Gunderson is a case in point. His homosexuality was never a secret in his district throughout his congressional career, and his overwhelming popularity and devotion to the interests of his rural constituents always assured him easy victory in a general election. But once his orientation became a matter of national media attention, he could never discount the possibility that the antigay party faction would oppose him in a primary contest focused primarily on that "issue." Thereby, ironically, the fundamentalist faction ultimately cost its party the district's House seat. When first elected, Gunderson had vowed to serve no more than ten years in Congress, but stayed on an extra three terms at the urging of party leaders who feared the district would go Democratic without him. Finally, in 1996, he reluctantly agreed to stand once more, but only if he had no opposition in the primary. When it became apparent that would not be the case, and that he would have to face a primary challenge concerned primarily with his sexual orientation, he went with his original decision to step down—and the district, as Republican leaders had feared, went Democratic.

Still, the eventual insignificance of orientation as a political factor was perhaps foreshadowed in the early years of the Republican administration of George W. Bush. A president never known as gay-friendly, and who has always relied heavily on his party's hard-core antigay wing, Bush nonetheless appointed at least thirty open gays to high- and middle-level administration jobs in his first two years as president, according to the Log Cabin Republicans, a gay political group.

One of those appointees took office on September 19, 2001, when Secretary of State Colin Powell presided over the swearing-in of career diplomat Michael Guest as United States Ambassador to Romania. Guest's partner of six years, Alex Nevarez, was acknowledged by Powell at the ceremony, and subsequently accompanied Guest to the Bucharest ambassadorial residence.

The Republican secretary's introduction of Nevarez was a small gesture. But it perhaps spoke volumes for the future of gays in public life.

12

A Holocaust Survivor Confronts Homophobia

In 2003, the United States Holocaust Memorial Museum ran an exhibition entitled "Nazi Persecution of Homosexuals." In what curator Edward Phillips described as their "draconian" effort to eradicate homosexuality, the Nazis arrested some 100,000 men, some of whom were castrated, while others died in concentration camps.

The exhibit for me recalled memories of a November evening a little more than two years after our first PFLAG meeting, when my wife, Myrna, and I attended a black-tie event in the elegant Grand Ballroom of New York's Waldorf-Astoria Hotel. At the head table sat Elie Wiesel, Nobel Peace laureate and world-renowned chronicler of the Holocaust. Next to him sat Paulette Goodman, the woman who had presided over our first PFLAG meeting. They were both being honored with Humanitarian Awards from the Human Rights Campaign, an organization dedicated to equality and justice for lesbians and gay men.

It was fitting in another way, too, for Paulette to share the spotlight with Wiesel. Both had lived through the Holocaust. And both were there that night largely because the persecution of lesbians and gay men evoked memories of that horrible era. In his keynote speech, Wiesel took note of the fact that gays shared with Jews the fate of Nazi death camps—that he personally had seen gays "in those places of darkness, silence, and fire."

He went on to supply the answer to a question on the minds of many of the eight hundred present: why would one of the most eminent scholars and writers of our age, himself from an orthodox religious background, accept an award from an organization of homosexual activists? "You need not be surprised," Wiesel said. "Those who hate you, hate me. Those who hate, hate everybody. So why should I not be here to speak to you about self-respect and about civil rights that must apply to every single segment of our population and to every area of human endeavors? We are all human beings."

In accepting her own award on behalf of PFLAG, of which she had been national president for the past year, Paulette cited her own memories of the Holocaust. She recalled her childhood in Nazi-occupied Paris, and told of the loss of numerous relatives in German death camps. To survive, she said, she had to hide the fact that she was a Jew: "I know how stifling it is to be in the closet."

Paulette was one of nine children of Polish parents who had moved to Paris when her father became an ironworker for the French national railroad. There, as a youngster during World War II, she was required to wear a Star of David on her clothing. Other children called her *sale Juive*, "dirty Jew."

Thus, as a young child, Paulette learned what it meant to be "different." Once a week, defying a Nazi order banning Jews from appearing in various public places, she would take off her Star of David and go with other children to the movies, "even though we knew that if we got caught, the whole family would have been wiped out."

A Holocaust Survivor Confronts Homophobia

She has no idea why most of her immediate family were spared the Gestapo dragnets that claimed aunts, uncles, nieces, nephews, and grandparents. But when the war ended, relatives in New York City helped Paulette, one sister, and two brothers emigrate there. Her parents were unable to obtain U.S. visas for themselves, and so moved to Montreal, where other relatives lived. The sixteen-year-old Paulette had never before been separated from her parents; after three months in New York, she decided to move to Montreal to be with them. Then, nine days before her departure, she met Leo Goodman, a nineteen-year-old engineering student.

A series of obstacles plagued the ensuing courtship. The first was language. Paulette's English was still halting. They both understood Yiddish, having heard it regularly in their childhood homes—but neither could speak it. At first, they had to communicate largely by hand signals, but their affection for each other was nonetheless clear by the time Paulette moved to Montreal. Thereafter, daily exchanges of letters and frequent trips by Paulette to New York and Leo to Montreal—one for several months while he worked there as a draftsman and toolmaker—kept the relationship going.

They became engaged, only to worry in their youthful innocence about still another potential barrier. In moving to Canada, Paulette had relinquished her immigrant status in the United States. Hesitantly, during a visit to New York in 1951, they entered an immigration office. A clerk sternly advised them that while wives of U.S. citizens were allowed in the country, mere betrothal conferred no standing whatever on Paulette. They were crestfallen. But the clerk winked. "It's simple," he said. "Just get married." Three days later, on a hot summer afternoon, they were married in the living room of a Yonkers judge. (Paulette didn't consider herself "really married" until a rabbi performed a second cere-mony some months later in a relative's home in Montreal.)

Paulette and Leo were together for more than forty years prior to his death in 1996, and she has two children and two grandchildren. Until the early 1980s, Paulette's energies went almost entirely into her family. She thought of herself as an old-fashioned homemaker, and had few out-side interests. Then, while living in Maryland, where Leo worked as a research scientist, they learned one of their children was gay.

Paulette, more distressed than Leo by the revelation, found a sup-port group composed of a handful of other parents and a few gay men. As she learned about homosexuality and the irrational animosity it aroused, she was reminded of the bigotry and hatred the Nazis had engendered.

As a child wearing her Star of David, Paulette had been unaware of the Nazi oppression of gays. Between 1933 and 1945, the Germans arrested as many as 100,000 gay men, jailed some 60,000, and sent 10,000 to 15,000 to concentration camps. In the prisons and camps, gays wore pink triangles on their sleeves. Like the Jews' yellow Star of David, it was homosexuals' particular badge of disgrace and dishonor. (Today, it carries a very different meaning; it has become the worldwide symbol of the gay liberation movement.)

Included in the permanent exhibit of the Holocaust Museum in Washington, D.C., are documents, photographs, and artifacts related to the Nazi treatment of gays; it was probably the world's first museum to include memorabilia of a gay community in a scholarly exhibit. Col-lecting the material has been complicated by the reluctance of most sur-vivors to speak of their experiences with researchers; many continued to find it difficult to think of themselves as anything other than common criminals. For one thing, in the wake of World War II, Germany was swept by moral crusades fueled by appeals to so-called family values, and many of the gay Holocaust survivors reportedly were again arrested and imprisoned.

Nazi persecution of gays was still unknown to Paulette in 1983, when she found herself edging into a leadership role in the fight against American prejudice. In that year, she and Leo decided to organize their little support group into the Washington-area chapter of PFLAG. She wanted Leo to be the first president, but he demurred and no one else stepped forward; by default, the position fell to Paulette.

Her activist career was launched, but it had a slow start. For the second time in her life, she found herself closeted. She shunned publicity of any sort. Although chapter meetings were held at her house, she never told her neighbors why all these people were visiting her. (She let them assume that the Goodmans gave a lot of parties.) She remembers several occasions when, hearing a neighbor at the door, she frantically hid any books or literature that might give her away. "I would be absolutely beside myself," she says. "This is what it's like being in the closet."

Ultimately, she was outed by the media after the chapter decided to sponsor an ad campaign on city buses to seek new members. A county councilman objected to the plan, and suddenly PFLAG was in the news. Paulette was called by a *Washington Post* reporter who had learned from a county document of her role as PFLAG president. Once the *Post* article appeared, television cameras were at her door. This time, hiding the books and literature could not help!

In retrospect, she is grateful for the outing. As head of Washington

PFLAG, she was responsible for getting the word out to others who needed support: "How could we reach out to people if I was not able to speak openly?" As it happened, she found speaking out to be personally liberating, and few since have found Paulette Goodman short of words or camera-shy where the welfare of "our gay loved ones" is at stake.

She has spoken before state and local legislatures, been featured in scores of newspaper and magazine articles, and has appeared on television and radio programs. She has led workshops at universities and churches, and at organizations (gay and non-gay) beyond count. On numerous occasions, she has gone jaw-to-jaw with antigay hardliners. Once, as television cameras whirred, she even debated a notorious antigay crusader, Reverend Joseph Chambers, on a city sidewalk.

That confrontation took place in 1991 in Charlotte, North Carolina, in front of the Omni Charlotte Hotel, site of that year's PFLAG national convention. For months prior to the convention, through the media and the newsletter of his own organization, known as Concerned Charlotteans, Chambers roused his supporters to a fever pitch of antigay sentiment. He told them that PFLAG's pro-family stance was a facade designed "to fool the public and hide its immoral deeds." The use of convention name tags, he said, was "a slick plan so homosexuals can make contact for sodomy sex." He also claimed that the inverted pink triangle was an occult symbol "frequently denoting the unholy trinity of Satan, the Antichrist, and the false prophet."

During the convention itself, Chambers's followers picketed the hotel with signs proclaiming, "The homosexual conference is not telling you the truth." Paulette happened to pass the picketers one afternoon when Chambers himself was present, and her temper flared. Within moments, the woman who not long before had hidden PFLAG literature from her neighbors was surrounded by television cameras and reporters as she denounced Chambers to his face. Charlotte viewers heard her on that night's newscast, sharply informing Chambers that it was antigay bigotry, not PFLAG, that was destroying families.

Of all her accomplishments, Paulette is probably proudest of the part she has played in educating mental health professionals on behalf of misunderstood gay and lesbian children. She has spoken, for example, at annual meetings of both the American Psychiatric Association and the American Academy of Child and Adolescent Psychiatry. It is the plight of lesbian and gay youth, evoking visions of her own frightened and closeted childhood, that now concerns her most.

Starting in 1988, Paulette led national PFLAG during four years of mush-rooming growth. When she took the reins, the organization was a loose confederation of local groups run out of her Maryland kitchen. When she stepped down in 1992, PFLAG was a national presence with more than three hundred chapters and hot lines in twelve countries, all admin-istered by a professional staff in Washington, D.C. In the next ten years, the number of affiliates would grow to more than 450.

During her tenure, while a conservative Republican administration was in power, she obtained recognition and support for PFLAG from within the White House itself. The incident, which triggered angry remonstrances from the conservative wing of the Republican party, reveals both Paulette's generosity of heart and her doggedness of purpose.

In 1989, impressed by the apparent warmth of First Lady Barbara Bush, Paulette wrote her a letter "mother-to-mother." In it, she asked Mrs. Bush to "speak kind words to some twenty-four million gay Americans and their families, to help heal the wounds, and to keep these families in loving relationships." Paulette was keenly disappointed when she received nothing more than a routine acknowledgment from a White House aide.

In April 1990, however, Paulette decided to try another tack. She and I were among those attending the signing of the Hate Crimes Statistics Act by President Bush, and Paulette brought along a copy of the 1989 letter. She asked me whether I thought she should give it to one of the White House staffers with the request that it be hand-delivered to Mrs. Bush.

"No harm in trying," I told her, although I wondered why she would want to waste her energy in such a patently useless way. After all, Bush was no political novice, and her husband had been elected on a strongly conservative platform.

Paulette followed her optimistic instincts, and ten days later received a note on White House stationery. "You sound like a caring parent and a compassionate citizen," the first lady began, and then added the words that warmed the hearts of PFLAGers around the country:

> I firmly believe that we cannot tolerate discrimination against any individuals or groups in our country. Such treatment always brings with it pain and perpetuates hate and intolerance. I appreciate so much your sharing the information about your organization and your encouraging me to help change attitudes. Your words speak eloquently of your love for your child and your compassion for all gay Americans and their families.
>
> With all best wishes, warmly, Barbara Bush.

The First Lady's gracious reply soon came to the attention of conservative Republicans, who immediately attacked the White House.

According to syndicated columnist Robert Novak, the critics found Mrs. Bush's simple expression of fair play to be an "outrage." The column described "Republican politicians and worried White House aides" as being concerned that the letter had "pushed the Bush agenda into political danger." Paulette herself was described as a "gay-lobby activist."

But Paulette had the last word, in remarks quoted in several newspapers, including the *Washington Post* and *Chicago Sun-Times*. Far from being a gay-lobby activist, she said, "I am simply the mother of two wonderful children, one of whom happens to be gay, and a volunteer in an organization dedicated to keeping families together.

"It was in those roles that I wrote Mrs. Bush, and she responded in a caring and nonpolitical vein. She apparently realizes that it is society's discrimination against our kids—and not their innate sexual orientation—that truly threatens family structures."

The undoubted apex of Paulette's PFLAG experience came after she retired as national president. On April 23, 1993, the United States Holocaust Memorial Museum was dedicated in the nation's capital. (Appropriately, perhaps, the dedication occurred during the week of a massive march on Washington for gay civil rights.) The speaker representing PFLAG was the woman who remembered having to remove her Star of David in order to go to the movies with other children in Paris.

As at the dinner in New York with Elie Wiesel two years earlier, Paulette compared her Holocaust experience with that of gays everywhere. "I and other French Jewish children had to fool the Christians so that we could survive," she said. "So I was denied my Yiddishkeit [Jewish identity]. Because of prejudice and oppression, I was not proud of being a Jew. But now I am proud to be a Jew, proud to be the parent of a gay child, and proud to be a member of PFLAG.

"At first when I found out I had a gay child, I found myself in a closet again, just as my child had been before coming out to us. So I realize the prejudice gay, lesbian, bisexual, and transgender people are living through. It did not take me long to see the parallels. Oppression and prejudice and persecution are the same wherever they occur."

The dedication crowd cheered in agreement. And it chanted, "Never again! Never again! Never again!"

13

A Survival Guide

Your child has just come out to you. What now?

If you're at all typical, you're not Jeanne Manford or Tom Potter, to whom the disclosure was no more shocking than being informed of their child's favorite singer. You're not Mary Griffith, for whom the revelation evoked visions of hellfire and damnation. You're not Mel Wheatley, who just "knew" that if his son was gay, the stereotypes must be wrong. Nor are you the mother in Houston who says, "When my son told me he was gay, I said, 'How can that be? You're a terrible dresser and you always have holes in your socks.' Every gay man I'd ever known was a snappy dresser."

Still, if you do not share her nonchalance and irony, you probably will share the Houston mother's disbelief. The most common parental reaction to the news is denial. You will probably run through a series of anxious disclaimers: "How can you be sure?" "You haven't dated enough boys (girls)." "This is just a phase you're going through." But by the time children have mustered the courage to come out to parents, they have probably resolved any doubt in their own minds. They are, after all, risking hurt or outright rejection, and are hardly likely to do so on a whim.

While you will need to take care of both yourself and your child, taking care of your son or daughter is the simpler part. No matter how heavy the emotional hit you have absorbed, presumably you still love your child. Children need to hear that. They need to know they are not being ejected from either home or heart—that is probably what they feared most about coming out to you. They don't expect praise and celebration. They know how difficult it was for *them* to accept the fact that they're gay, and they are probably prepared to give you time and help to do the same. But they need to know they're still part of the family.

Taking care of yourself can be more complicated. This is especially true if the news comes as a complete surprise, if you've never even considered the possibility of having a gay child. You might feel terrible grief, as if your child had just died. Parents often liken the experience to losing a loved one, frequently passing through similar stages of grief. This seems to happen because in a sense there *has* been a death—of the image of the child that you cherished in your mind.

And grief is just one of the unsettling feelings you might experience. Some of the others are guilt ("What did I do wrong?"), shame ("What will my friends think?"), and anger ("How could you do this to me?"). Whatever form the pain takes, you won't help yourself by suppressing or denying it. It's real, it's normal, and for now you're entitled to it. But you shouldn't have to bear the burden alone. Tell your child that you'd like to discuss the situation with someone you trust: one or more close friends, perhaps, or a minister or rabbi. Tell them what you are feeling but don't look for magic cures or profound wisdom. Their value right now is simply as sympathetic listeners, outlets for your woe.

Above all, it's important to talk. Some parents carry the burden in silence for years; most of them will tell you it's a brutal form of self-punishment.

You might strike gold in the form of a confidante who has a relative or close friend who is gay, and who can provide you with some truly meaningful insights. But don't count on it. Misinformation on this subject is still rife in our society.

Often, parents fear that telling their good friends might damage their relationships. Judging by the scores of parents I've talked to, that's unlikely. If anything, your friends may be overly sympathetic, tacitly buying into the notion that you and your family have suffered some sort of tragedy. And while an occasional acquaintance might tend to think less of you—well, most parents eventually conclude that such a person wasn't worth calling "friend" anyway.

Desperately seeking someone to "blame"—yourself, your spouse, your child's friends, the schools, the media—is another typical, but wholly unwarranted, response to a child's coming out. While research is beginning to provide some clues, no one yet knows what "causes" homosexuality. But one thing that is certain is that poor parenting is not the cause. Nor do children choose to be gay. As writer Richard Mohr points out, picking the gender of a sex partner is quite different from picking a flavor of ice cream. "If people were persecuted, threatened with jail terms, shattered careers, and loss of family and housing and the like for eating, say, Rocky Road ice cream, no one would ever eat it."

Ultimately, you are apt to decide that any notion of blame is inappropriate in this situation—that sexual orientation is no more fit an object of stigma than is hair color or taste in music. In all likelihood, your child has simply recognized a significant facet of his or her personality, the denial of which would jeopardize the attainment of personal well-being.

The experience of coming out to oneself is a matter of discovery, of peeling away layers of denial and shame. Coming out to you is an act of courage on your child's part. It is also a demonstration of trust in you. Someday, if not now, you'll be grateful for that.

If you can't shake the sense that disaster has struck, be assured that time can do more than merely ease the pain. It can erase it and actually replace it with joy. To that end, seek out the nearest PFLAG hot line or support group. If there's none listed in your telephone directory, call the national office (202-467-8180). At PFLAG, you'll find caring and understanding—the type of support available only from those who know what you're going through because they have been there themselves. And you'll find the comfort and warmth of solid new friendships.

In a short time, moreover, you will become something of an expert in an area in which most Americans know very little. You may not be out of the closet yet, but you will know that a lot of things other people say about homosexuality are just rumor, innuendo, or misinformation. "Suddenly you're smart in an area where most of the people in the country are just plain dumb," says psychotherapist Cathy Tuerk. "So it helps your self-esteem."

At PFLAG meetings, you'll also meet lesbians and gay men, and nothing dispels the myths about homosexuality more quickly than meeting people who are ordinary and likable and gay. Through them, you'll gain significant insight into what it's like to grow up gay—and to have to deal with parents who, like you, are unprepared to handle that. Chances are, the experience will increase your respect for your own child.

There are a number of helpful books with up-to-date objective information about homosexuality. Many libraries are expanding their collections on the subject, and PFLAG can provide you with appropriate titles. (See Appendix for a list of recommended readings.) But your most meaningful education will probably come from the people you will meet through PFLAG: other parents, and lesbians and gay men who confound all the stereotypes.

One father at a support group described the process this way: "I see all of us climbing a mountain. The higher we climb, the more we can see. But we're all at different levels. I think I'm somewhere in the middle of the mountain. I started from ignorance, and I still have a long way to go. But I can see much more now than from the bottom of the hill."

At some point in the process, you may become aware that you and your child have reversed roles. You will probably be traveling much the same tortuous path your child has already taken—and now, your child can teach you. He or she can help you learn what it means—and what it does not mean—to be gay, and can help you see the absurdity of many of your lifelong beliefs about homosexuality. Your child can help you understand how rewarding it is for you to look beyond social norms and simply be yourself. (As the song "I've Gotta Be Me" puts it, "How can I ever be right for somebody else if I'm not right for me?")

And yes, we even learn more about sexuality itself. For many parents, the most disturbing aspect of a child's homosexuality is imagining their sexual behavior. "I can't bear to think about what they do in the bedroom" is a common support-group lament.

If that's a concern to you, consider some statistics. The boudoir behavior of our gay and lesbian kids, it turns out, is not necessarily all that different from that of their heterosexual siblings. Studies reported by the Kinsey Institute in 1990 indicated that 90 percent of heterosexual couples had engaged in oral sex, and more than a third of American women had had anal sex. A later study reported lower, but still significant, incidences of these practices. Yet, it rarely occurs to us to wonder what our heterosexual children might be doing in *their* bedrooms.

"One of the things I find particularly galling," says Mitzi Henderson, a former PFLAG national president, "is the representation of gay people as being interested in sex as if that's the only thing that's important in their lives. Whenever they're talked about, it's in terms of sexual behavior. And yet when we talk about heterosexual people, we don't talk about adult book stores, prostitution, the sex lives of rock stars, as being typical of heterosexual people."

For those who have not had occasion to consider the prevalence of homosexuality, statistics can afford further surprise. The percentage of Americans who are gay and lesbian is a matter of some controversy. For many years, based on figures contained in the 1948 Kinsey report, the proportion was commonly assumed to be about 10 percent. More recent polls have placed the percentage lower, including at least one that pegged it at a mere 1 percent. Of course, polls have built-in biases: in a society where it is dangerous to be gay, it is not easy to admit homosexuality even to oneself, much less to an inquiring stranger. Most serious researchers—such as those at the Johns Hopkins School of Medicine, where some of the most intensive studies of homosexuality have taken place—estimate the incidence to be at least six percent.

Accepting this latter figure as the best available guess, and based on 2000 census figures, the number of gay people in the country is nearly seventeen million. Necessarily, those seventeen million began life with thirty-four million parents; and they have approximately seventeen million siblings. Their cousins, aunts, uncles, grandparents, and non-gay friends add up to further millions.

Thus, how we as families and as a society deal with homosexuality is not a narrow concern. It's a fair guess that something like half of all Americans have a reasonably direct stake in the issue. And while tens of thousands of them have taken advantage of PFLAG support and education resources, tens of *millions* have not.

Of these millions, some are unaware that their child, relative, or friend is gay. Others know or suspect, but prefer to deal with the matter in silence. And many simply have no need for special support, because they are not uncomfortable that someone close to them is gay.

Of those who do find their way to PFLAG, only a relatively small percentage become activists. Not surprisingly, the typical PFLAG member is not a Jeanne Manford, Mary Griffith, Bonnie or Buzz Frum, or Elise or Jim Self. To be sure, thousands march in annual gay-pride parades around the country as a gesture of parental support, and increasing numbers are speaking out against antigay discrimination in radio and television interviews, in their churches, and before city councils, school boards, state legislatures, and community agencies.

But most attend a few PFLAG meetings and then go on with their lives, their initial concerns lessened or eliminated. They are merely part of a silent army of decent, fair-minded, family-centered citizens. Most people, perhaps an overwhelming majority, are not cut out for activism. But parents of gay children, it seems to me, can't help but harbor at least a degree of righteous anger at those who would diminish their children. My hope is that the anger will someday surface, that the now-silent masses will stand up and make themselves heard.

It's understandable—perhaps inevitable—that parents suffer shock and grief when they first learn of a child's homosexuality. Fathers in particular often find it difficult to express support for a group of citizens commonly derided as "pansies." But their gay kids are in constant jeopardy from a hostile society. Hence, many of these fathers are eventually moved by the parental imperative to stand up for their own.

Jim Pines of Chevy Chase, Maryland, is a thoughtful man who is offended by macho posturing. He says he went through the usual denial, grieving, and other stages so familiar to parents of gay kids. But then came another response, which Jim believes is healthier. It was a combativeness, the fierceness of which astonished him. "In the same way I had always pictured a lion, for example, defending its cubs against the hunter, I found myself enraged that some people might attack my son, verbally or even physically, for something as private and unobjectionable as his sexual orientation.

"I continue to mask my rage, being too 'civilized' to act on it. But I consider my fierce reaction far more appropriate to my masculinity than lamenting my son's homosexuality."

The richest payoffs from adjusting to a child's gayness, however, come in more homespun form.

Pat Romero's face softens as she tells me about her family's affection for Mike Bieri, her gay son Mick's mate of twelve years. She calls the men's relationship a marriage, and Mike her son-in-law. In actuality, Pat's bond with Mike often seems more that of mother than mother-in-law. His own mother died when he was four, and he has few memories of her. So although Pat is close to the husbands of her two older daughters, there is an added dimension to her relationship with Mike. "I get more hugs from him than I do from Mick," she says.

The closeness of their relationship was never more apparent than when Mick became infatuated with another young man and for a brief time considered breaking up with Mike. Mick asked Pat to talk with

Mike about the situation, and they met over coffee. Mike's "dear blue eyes welled up with tears," Pat recalls, as he described how much it meant to him "to come home and there's Mick." But he said what hurt even more was that he wasn't only losing Mick, "I'm losing my family." When Pat passed this on to Mike's three sisters and their husbands, each told Mike that no matter what happened, he would remain part of the family. Indeed, Pat urged Mike to resist Mick's separation plans, which upset Mick. But she told Mick, "You just said talk to him. You didn't tell me what kind of advice I was supposed to give him."

"Our other daughter, when she comes over with her boyfriend, we expect them to hold hands, snuggle up. If Gina had a lover here, this is her house, she should be accorded the same rights."

Brian Leonard, stepfather of Gina Gutierrez, spoke at the kitchen table where he was sitting with Gina's mother, Gloria. Gina, then a senior at Los Gatos High School, was perched on a countertop, legs dangling. Gina had long before told her family she was gay, and a year earlier had made the disclosure to the entire school when she performed a monologue about coming out in the high school auditorium. Now, however, Gloria was having reservations about Gina dating other girls while still in high school, and Brian sought to reassure his wife. Placing his hand on hers, he observed gently, "Honey, this is the time kids *are* dating."

This intimate scene is part of a powerful documentary called *Gay Youth*, produced by Pam Walton, which has won eight awards and has been shown at film festivals around the world. It features eight gay adolescents, but tiny Gina—high-spirited and elfin, yet thoughtful, articulate, and resolute—is its unquestioned star. And Brian and Gloria fill, as it were, key supporting roles. It is clear that her parents' willingness to accept and appreciate her for who she is is crucial to Gina's confidence, courage, and winning personality.

Some months after the kitchen discussion, Gloria and Gina went shopping for a gown for Gina's senior prom, held in San Francisco. On prom night, Walton filmed Gina and three of her friends in a hotel room they were sharing to dress for the evening.

Gina's date was Cristina Salat. The other two seniors were Gina's close friend Julie Maxson and her date, Neil Laslett. In the film, Gina and Cristina are shown comparing their outfits and laughing about how "femme" they will look. Then, while Gina applies polish to Julie's nails, Julie speaks to the camera about her schoolmate. She doesn't think of Gina as a lesbian, she says, but simply as "Gina my friend." And she praises Gina's openness about her orientation. "I don't know if I could do something like that." The prom-night vignette ends with a shot of Gina and Cristina's formal photograph: two elegantly gowned young women, beaming before a festive backdrop of brightly colored balloons.

The film's climax focuses on Gina's graduation. At the awards ceremony, Brian and Gloria watch proudly as Gina receives a $500 scholarship award for her work with gay and lesbian issues. (The award, cosponsored by PFLAG and a Bay Area gay teachers group, was named in memory of Mary Griffith's son Bobby.) Then, at commencement, as she strode across the platform to receive her diploma, the announcement of her name triggered a noisy ovation from her fellow students.

At the end, the camera catches a teary Gina in long embraces with her mother and stepfather. Then they all burst into laughter as Gina reveals that she had been given a blank diploma: "I forgot to turn in a textbook."

A member of my PFLAG chapter, a white-haired former elementary school teacher, likes to talk about her living arrangement. Like many other older single women, she lives in a cozy mother-in-law apartment in her son's Victorian house.

That her son's partner is another man does not make these circumstances any less ordinary. She and the couple go pretty much their separate ways, following her golden rule of intergenerational living: "I don't smother them, and they don't smother me." But the men are there to help her with heavy tasks, she takes pleasure in doing occasional household errands for them while they're at work, and dinner together in her apartment is a ritual on holidays.

Friends regularly urge her to move to a nearby retirement development, with its broad range of senior activities. But she likes being with her family. She loves "my two sons," who have lived together for twenty years and spend much of their spare time working on the stately old Victorian house they have owned since 1977. She is fond of the tree-lined block of trim turn-of-the-century houses on which they live, with its friendly neighbors and many youngsters. (A lover of children, but with no grandchildren of her own, she counts herself "the third grandmother" of numerous tots.) And she's available when the men are looking for company at a movie or some special gathering.

"It's a comfortable arrangement," she says. "I can't imagine myself living anywhere else."

Straight from the Heart is an Academy Award-nominated video produced by Dee Mosbacher (see Chapter 10) and Frances Reid. One of the film's emotional highlights is a spontaneous outburst of affection in which Mildred Washington's twin daughters, both lesbian, smother her in hugs and kisses and peals of laughter. The playful display is touched off by

Mildred's obviously heartfelt tribute to Sandra and Sharon. "I'm very proud of my daughters," she says. "There is nothing they have ever done that I am not proud of." Pausing to look at them, she adds, "I'm proud of their accomplishments. I'm proud of their independence. I'm proud of the way they have always respected me and other adults and people their own age. I'm just proud of my daughters. I think they're the two most wonderful people in the world."

The Washingtons are African-American, a fact that complicated family acceptance of the girls' lesbianism. Some relatives saw homosexuality as "a white disease" and said the twins must have picked it up from white people. Others insisted that American blacks cannot be gay, since they're all descended from slaves chosen for strength, virility, and child-bearing capacity.

The twins' father, moreover, was a Hall of Fame miler at Ohio State who spent thirty years with the Department of Defense—a background that left him quite unprepared to accept gay children. But Donald Washington also loved young people—he spent most of his spare time in volunteer youth work—and had become enthusiastically supportive of his daughters for some years before his death in 1990.

To Mildred, a retired guidance counselor, acceptance was ultimately just a matter of common sense. Learning of the girls' orientation disturbed her. But was it a problem because they were gay, she asked herself, or because she was ashamed to tell her friends? "And all the answers came back to, the problem lies with me, not them."

The twins, thirty-four at the time of the filming, had indeed given Mildred much to be proud of. Sandra was a planner with the National Park Service in Lincoln, Nebraska. Sharon was a professor at Kent State. Together, they formed a professional singing team popular at African-American and gay community events for over a decade. Each was on the telephone with Mildred at least three times a week.

Being gay does not affect innate longings associated with ritual and tradition. Mildred's eyes twinkle as she recalls, "As a kid, Sandra always had a hope chest." And several months after the documentary was filmed, Sandra fulfilled her long-standing dream—she and her mate of five years, Deb Cirksena, were formally united in a church ceremony. A Congregational minister did the honors, and family members on both sides attended. Sharon was Sandra's best woman, and Mildred sang a duet with Deb's mother, a medley of "I Believe" and "Ave Maria."

By 2003, announcements of gay commitment ceremonies were being accepted and run by more than 180 mainstream newspapers, as well as in gay community publications in every major city. The rites have no legal standing, but that hardly lessens the joy of the accompanying celebrations. And increasingly, parents and other family members are among the celebrants, echoing Mildred Washington's pronouncement about her daughter's rites: "It was a wonderful, wonderful ceremony."

Pat and Dan Stone's 1994 Christmas card was a family portrait taken on the porch of their ranch home in Dallas. It showed Pat, Dan, and son Brad standing, grinning, behind the porch swing. Seated on the swing were daughter TJ and her partner, Katherine Allen. On the young women's laps were the Stones' two grandsons: Matt, seven, and Zack, born just eight months before.

The accompanying four-page letter from Dan explained that Matt was Katherine's son by an earlier marriage and that Zack was the Stones' first biological grandchild. TJ and Katherine had been together for six years; Zack's biological father, Keith Hyatte, was the thirteen year partner of Katherine's brother, John Allen. Keith had no legal or financial responsibility for Zack, but he and John considered themselves part of the family. "Of course," Dan wrote, "when TJ told us that she intended to get pregnant, she had to slow down and explain a lot of this to me."

Dan said his message was written for those friends who might not already be aware of the Stones' extended family. He explained, "By sending this letter with each card, everyone knows that everyone else has been posted. This may make it a little easier for you to open a discussion about the subject with others. There's no need to be secretive about this; we're certainly not."

When she was younger, TJ had told her parents that she wasn't going to "marry some guy and move far away." She kept part of the promise—she moved far away (to Virginia), but with a woman.

"And quite a woman she is," Dan wrote in his letter. "Katherine is a warm, caring person, a university professor and the loving life-partner of TJ. When the law allows it, they'll be married. We love Katherine and Matt and accept them as full members of our family. We benefit from their love."

Dan's message pointed out that gay people are often denied their full rights as citizens. However hard it is to comprehend, he wrote, gays are losing their jobs and even being killed, simply because they are gay:

> I hope you get the message. It's one that shouldn't be put in the closet. It needs talking about. I care about what you think or I would never have sent you this letter. I love my daughter, and I admire her and have been enriched by her life experiences. I accept her without any reservation, and I want you to accept her and her

family with the warmth that you have always extended to me.
That's my Christmas wish.

These families have overcome the impediments raised by social prejudice—
and the best gauge of their victory is the ordinariness with which they
view their gay family members. We like to feel that's the way it is in our
family, too.

My daughter Bobbi has been in a committed relationship since
1989 with Donna Hylton, a systems analyst living in suburban Washington, D.C. For Myrna and me, and for Bobbi's mother and grandmother, embracing a same-sex couple in the family circle was hardly an
immediate response. But our adjustment to what now seems commonplace was aided by the relaxed attitudes of our other children. Unlike
most older people, many of today's young adults have known gay people
in school, work, and social settings; to them, the gender of a loved one's
mate can be a matter of little moment. Fortunately, for us, that's how it
was with Bobbi's siblings.

Thanks to them and their mates, Bobbi and Donna are just another
of the couples in our family—no big deal. Bobbi's closest friend has
always been her older sister, Sharon. Both daughters have always related
to Myrna's two sons, Douglas and Dietrich Nebert, as brothers rather
than stepbrothers. And Bobbi's coming out produced nary a ripple in
any of the relationships.

Bobbi is now a civil rights prosecutor for the Department of Justice.
Doug and Dietrich are both married and have children of their own.

While at Stanford Law School, Bobbi spent virtually every
weekend with Sharon and her future husband, John Sheehan, who were
then living in nearby Oakland. Frequently, Donna would fly in to visit

Bobbi, and all four of the young people would get together. One Thanksgiving, they were joined by Dietrich, then single and living in Oregon, who drove six hundred miles to stay with Bobbi and share the holiday with her, Donna, Sharon, and John. On Thanksgiving Day, they all pitched in to prepare dinner at Sharon and John's. Then they all got sick together, apparently because the oven malfunctioned and the turkey was undercooked. But the "turkey trot," as they called it, has become part of family lore—the kind of shared adversity that somehow, over time, becomes amusing.

If Bobbi and Donna are just another pair in the extended clan, they have nevertheless added an important dimension to our family calculus.

For one thing, Bobbi and Donna are the only couple for whom the rest of the family regularly feels moved to express public support. One way we do this is by marching in gay-pride parades. The throng of Bobbi's relatives usually includes her grandmother and even, in one instance, Doug's then nine-month-old son, Corey.

The mere presence of Bobbi and Donna within the family circle has other effects. For example, Doug and his wife, Dee Ann, say that Bobbi and Donna serve a kind of special education function for their three children. For however hate-free a home might be, youngsters cannot wholly avoid society's antigay cast. So when their daughter, then twelve, expressed disapproval about a gay couple in a movie, Dee Ann and Doug had a ready response. They reminded her that her own family includes such a pair, Bobbi and Donna, whom she likes and admires.

Of course, when I proclaim the ordinariness of having a gay couple in the family, I'm engaging in a certain amount of self-contradiction. If it really were ordinary, I wouldn't be writing about it. Marching in support of the rights of Bobbi and Donna would have no more meaning than marching for those of Sharon and John, Doug and Dee Ann, or Dietrich and his wife, Allison. Dan Stone would have felt no need to send a four-page explanation with his Christmas card. Mildred Washington's motherly declaration of pride in her two daughters would merit a mere shrug rather than inclusion in a documentary.

Still, our experiences, and those of countless others, prove that gay children can fit seamlessly into the family circle. However strong your initial shock, you'll probably soon realize that your son or daughter is the same person he or she was before coming out to you—as worthy of your love now as before. You may need some help to get to the point of easy acceptance—from PFLAG or some other sympathetic source—but you can get there. And when you arrive, you and your family will be whole once more.

14

A Call to Arms

Vic Basile's father, Jimmy Basile, was a Catholic Italian-American, a second-generation party precinct worker in an industrialized New England neighborhood. Vic says that "fits a stereotype of someone you might think would be a bigot." And indeed, when Vic came out to his parents in 1981, Jimmy seemed to go into shock. Although his mother was instantly supportive, "for Dad it was pure trauma."

The love of politics runs in the family. Vic was the first executive director of an organization now known as the Human Rights Campaign, the nation's leading gay lobbying group and a powerful player on the national political scene. An important turning point in his father's attitude toward gay people was a black-tie organizational dinner in Washington, D.C., to which Vic invited his parents. Vic knew that Jimmy still harbored some stubborn stereotypes, and he hoped that the sight of hundreds of successful, well-dressed lesbians and gay men from all professions and careers might help change those images.

Vic was nervous about one matter. He warned his parents they would be seeing something new for them: the sight of men greeting each other by kissing. "Mother said, 'OK, fine,'" Vic remembers. "But Dad said nothing. I could see he was edgy about it. That made me even jumpier."

At the dinner, father and son were both tense for the first few minutes as Vic began introducing Jimmy to his acquaintances. Then, after about the fourth person, Jimmy kissed every man Vic introduced him to!

Jimmy had a grand time that night. He even met one of his longtime political heroes, openly gay Massachusetts congressman Barney Frank. And some months later came a vivid demonstration of how Jimmy's feelings about Vic's gayness had changed. Jimmy was interviewed for a newspaper feature story about his longtime political activity, and he made a special point of telling the reporter to write how proud he was of his gay son.

The sentiment was roundly returned. Vic's voice catches as he tells that story about the change in attitude of a "very Catholic" elderly man with a macho ethnic heritage. "It was very touching for me to see this happen," Vic says. "It's a very remarkable thing he did."

Icy stereotypes have a way of thawing when exposed to real-life openly gay and lesbian people. The same point was made by Mel Wheatley to his fellow bishops and by Wayne Schow to his fellow Mormons (chapter 9): homosexuality isn't about morals or theology, it's about people. Very frequently, they are people who are vital, creative, caring, and interesting—people you feel fortunate, sometimes even honored, to know. When you meet them, the stereotypes suddenly no longer make sense. And if you get to know them well, it can even change your life.

Not long after my introduction to PFLAG, my earlier prejudice toward gay people was turned on its head. I came to believe that many of them were better people for being openly gay—for daring to be themselves. It's like the point of an old Hasidic story about a Rabbi Zusya, who went to heaven expecting to be asked, "Why weren't you more like Moses?" Instead, he was asked, "Why weren't you more like Rabbi Zusya?"

As parents of gay children, we have the privilege of sharing in the triumphs and setbacks of young people as they confront the challenge of being themselves. We admire their courage in facing up to it. And we are warmed by the aura of joy that accompanies their success.

Moreover, as the stories in this book illustrate, parents often experience a similar sense of liberation. For we face our own challenges and fears, the overcoming of which can lead to new levels of sensitivity and self-awareness. The words *joy* and *liberation* are spoken often by parents as well as gays to describe their life-changing experiences.

I heartily second Mel Wheatley's observation that his life has been incredibly enriched by knowing gay and lesbian people. I know that society's lingering cruelty will cause hardships for my daughter. But a life without struggle is hardly worth the name. And her struggle will be shared with a community that is long on wisdom, warmth, and compassion.

Perhaps I shouldn't ask for more. But I do. Expanding awareness has brought impatience:

- Impatience with school officials who deny teenagers the courses and counseling that could save them from despair, addiction, and death.
- Impatience with state laws that treat a substantial minority of their citizens as second-class citizens or worse.
- Impatience with the hypocrisy of some churches and church leaders who preach love but practice oppression.

- Impatience with a military system that wastes taxpayer money while scarring the lives of able, brave Americans.
- Impatience with politicians at every level who allow their votes to be swayed by demagogues of bigotry.
- And, yes, I confess, impatience with parents who are slow to speak out on behalf of their gay and lesbian children.

Shortly after my daughter Bobbi told me she was a lesbian, I had a dream. It was a dream of an uprising of tens of millions of parents insisting on an end to society's cruelty toward their gay kids. Instinctual parental love, I thought, would inevitably lead these legions to reject the nonsense that clutters the national mindset. It would, I reasoned, quickly convert them to crusaders for justice and the celebration of cultural diversity. The result, I envisioned, would be a sea change in social attitudes toward homosexuality and gay people.

Sixteen years later, I sometimes have difficulty keeping the dream in focus.

To be sure, a cadre of uncloseted and sometimes outspoken parents does exist, and its numbers, however slowly, are growing. As I write, for example, PFLAG has more than 450 affiliates throughout the country. We shall overcome. But the moment of triumph is considerably farther down the road, and more difficult of achievement, than my first flush of enthusiasm led me to believe.

Too often, it turns out that the force of parental love is simply no match for that of societal bigotry. Many parents of gay kids are themselves so oppressed—by religious traditions, by their own inner sexual terrors, by peer pressure—that they shrink from personal enlightenment as from some dread demon. In gratuitous panic and rage, they disown their gay children.

Or by a type of spiritual dismissal that is just as hurtful, they simply refuse to acknowledge an important part of their children's well being.

Others, while more enlightened, profess not to see the importance of taking a public stand. They are perhaps personally accepting of their children's gayness, and acknowledge the falsity of conventional stereotypes. Nevertheless, they are unwilling to pay the price—vastly inflated in their minds—of leaving their relatively comfortable closets. For them, the craving for peer approval may command a higher priority. The imagined responses of others can carry the day.

I don't rule out the possibility, though, that the single most important factor may simply be the old enemy—apathy—fed by a lack of awareness of the impact that every parent can make.

The oppression of our children is kept alive in large part by the big lie. In their book *After the Ball*, Marshall Kirk and Hunter Madsen define this as the widespread assumption that gays are "rare freaks." This is the notion that homosexuality, while a product of sin and/or sickness, is nevertheless sufficiently rare that it can be ignored by "proper" folk.

If the big lie is to be countered, parents of gay children must play a key role. The prejudice of centuries won't be eliminated overnight, but it cannot long survive a concerted challenge by those of us with gay loved ones.

Do you have a gay child, relative, or friend? Enlist in the fight to unmask the big lie.

You have nothing to lose but a musty, uncomfortable closet.

Appendix

Following is a list of recommended resources for parents and for gay, lesbian and bisexual persons.

Parents, Families and Friends of Lesbians and Gays (PFLAG)

1726 M St. NW, Suite 400
Washington, DC 20036
Phone: 202-467-8180 (To order publications or to find a chapter near you, dial extention 210)
Fax: 202-467-8194
E-mail: info@pflag.org
Web site: www.pflag.org

Other National Organizations
Advocates for Youth
1025 Vermont Ave., N.W., Ste. 200
Washington, DC 20005
202–347–5700
info@advocatesforyouth.org
www.youthresource.com

BiNet USA
1800 Market St., Ste. 405
San Francisco, CA 94102
415–865–5628
BiNetUSA@aol.com

Bisexual Resource Center
P.O. Box 1026
Boston, MA, 02117-1026
617–424–9595
brc@biresource.org

Children of Lesbians and Gays Everywhere
3543 18th St., #1
San Francisco, CA 94110
415–861–KIDS
colage@colage.org

Gay Asian Pacific Support network
P.O. Box 461104
Los Angeles, CA 90046
213–368–6488

Gay and Lesbian Alliance Against Defamation
150 West 26th Street, Suite 503
New York, NY 10001
212–807–1700
www.glaad.org

Gay and Lesbian Medical Association
459 Fulton St., Ste. 107
San Francisco, CA 94102
415–255–4547
info@glma.org

Gay and Lesbian Parents Coalition International
P. O. Box 50360
Washington, DC 20091
202–583–8029
www.GLPCI.org

Gay, Lesbian and Straight Education Network
122 W. 26th Street, Suite 1100
New York, NY 10001
212–721–0135
www.glsen.org

Hetrick-Martin Institute for Lesbian and Gay Youth
2 Astor Place
New York, NY 10003
212–647–2400
www.hmi.org

Mautner Project for Lesbians with Cancer
1707 L ST., N.W., Ste. 230
Washington, DC 20036
202–332–5536
mautner@mautnerproject.org

National Association of Lesbian, Gay, Bisexual & Transgender Community Centers
208 W. 13th St. New York, NY 10011
212–620–7310
info@gaycenter.org

National Association of People With AIDS
1413 K St., N.W., 8th floor
Washington, DC 20005
202–898–0414
napwa@napwa.org

National Black Lesbian and Gay Leadership Forum
1714 Franklin St., Ste. 100-140
Oakland, CA 94612
510–302–0930

National Center for Lesbian Rights
870 Market St., Ste. 570
San Francisco, CA 94102
415–392–6257
info@nclrights.org

National Gay and Lesbian Task Force
1700 Kalorama Road, N.W.
Washington, DC 20009-2624
202–332–6483
TTY 202–332–6219
ngltf@ngltf.org

LLEGÓ-National Latina/o Lesbian, Gay, Bisexual & Transgender
    Organization
1420 K St., N. W., Ste. 200
Washington, DC 20006
202–408–5380

Servicemembers Legal Defense Network
P.O. Box 65301
Washington, DC 20035-5301
Phone: 202–328–3244
Web site: sldn@sldn.org

Sexuality Information and Education Council of the United States
130 W. 42nd St., Suite 350
New York, NY 10036-7802
Phone: 212–819–9770
Web site: siecus@siecus.org

Sexual Minority Youth Assistance League (SMYAL)
410 7th Street SE
Washington, D.C. 20003-2707

Phone: 202-546-5940

Religious Organizations
Affirmation (Mormon)
P.O. Box 33532
Washington, D.C. 20033

Affirmation (United Methodist)
P.O. Box 1021
Evanston, IL 60204
Phone: 847-733-9590

Al-Faitha Foundation (Muslim)
405 Park Ave, Suite 1500
New York, NY 10022
Phone: 212-752-4242

Association of Welcoming and Affirming Baptists
P.O. Box 2596
Attleboro Falls, MA 02763-0894
Phone: 508-226-1945

Brethren/Mennonite Council for Lesbian and Gay Concerns
P.O. Box 6300
Minneapolis, MN 55406
Phone: 612-722-6906

Dignity/USA (Catholic)
1500 Massachusetts Ave., N.W., Suite 11
Washington, D.C. 20005-1894
Phone: 1-800-877-8797

Emergence International (Christian Scientist)
P.O. Box 26237
Phoenix, AZ 85068
Phone: 1-800-280-6653

Evangelicals Concerned with Reconciliation
P.O. Box 19734
Seattle, WA 98109-6734
Phone: 206-621-8960

Gay Buddhist Fellowship
2215-R Market St., PMB456
San Franciso, CA 94114
Phone: 415-974-9878

Integrity (Episcopalian)
1718 M St., N.W.
P.O. Box 148
Washington, D.C. 20036
Phone: 1-800-462-9498

Lutherans Concerned
P.O. Box 1022
Indianapolis, IN 46206-1922

More Light Presbyterians
PMB 246A
4737 County Rd. 101
Minnetonka, MN 55345-2634

National Gay Pentecostal Alliance
P.O. Box 20428
Ferndale, MI 48220

Office of GLBT Concerns for Unitarian Universalists Association
25 Beacon St.
Boston, MA 02108
Phone: 617-948-6475

SDA Kinship International (Seventh-Day Adventist)
P.O. Box 7320
Laguna Nigel, CA 92607
949-248-1299

United Fellowship of Metropolitan Community Churches
8704 Santa Monica Blvd., 2nd Floor
West Hollywood, CA 90069
Phone: 310-360-8640

Unity Fellowship Church Movement (African American)
5148 West Jefferson Blvd.
Los Angeles, CA 90016

World Congress of Gay, Lesbian, Bisexual and Transgender Jews
P.O. Box 23379
Washington, D.C. 20026-3379
Phone: 202-452-7424

Hotlines

Gay and Lesbian National Hotline
1-888-843-GLNH (4564)

National AIDS Hotline
1-800-342-AIDS (2437)
1-800-344-7432 (Spanish)
1-800-243-7889 (TTY)

National Gay and Lesbian Youth Hotline
1-800-347-TEEN (8336)

The Trevor Hotline
1-800-850-8078

Recommended reading for parents, family, and friends:

Always My Child: A Parent's Guide to Understanding Your Gay, Lesbian, Bisexual, Transgendered, or Questioning Son or Daughter, Kevin Jennings, Fireside, 2002.

And Say Hi to Joyce: The Life and Chronicles of a Lesbian Couple, Deb Price and Joyce Murdoch. Doubleday, 1995.

Are You Still My Mother? Gloria Guss Back. Warner Books, 1985.

Beyond Acceptance, Carolyn Griffin and Marian and Arthur Wirth. Prentice-Hall, 1986.

Different Daughters: A Book by Mothers of Lesbians, Louise Rafkin. Cleis Press, 1987.

Family: A Portrait of Gay and Lesbian America, Nancy Andrews. Harper San Francisco, 1994.

Hearing Us Out: Voices from the Gay and Lesbian Community, Roger Sutton. Little, Brown and Company, 1994.

Homosexuality: The Secret A Child Dare Not Tell, Mary Ann Cantwell. Rafael Press, 1996.

Loving Someone Gay: Revised and Updated, Don Clark, Ph.D. Signet Books, 1987.

My Son Eric, Mary V. Borhek. The Pilgrim Press, 1979.

Now That You Know: What Every Parent Should Know About Homosexuality, Betty Fairchild and Nancy Hayward. Harcourt Brace Javanovich, 1989.

Parents Matter, Ann Muller. Naiad Press, 1987.

Prayers for Bobby: A Mother's Coming to Terms With the Suicide of Her Gay Son, Leroy Aarons. Harper San Francisco, 1995

The Family Heart: A Memoir of When Our Son Came Out, Robb Forman Dew. Ballantine Books, 1995. Audiotape available from Simon & Schuster.

238

Recommended reading on religion and homosexuality

Can Homophobia Be Cured? Wrestling with Questions that Challenge the Church, Bruce Hilton. Abington Press, 1992.

Homosexuality and Religion, Richard Hasbany, editor. Haworth Press, 1990.

In God's Image; Christian Witness to the Need for Gay/Lesbian Equality in the Eyes of the Church, Robert Warren Cromey. Alamo Square Press, San Francisco, 1991.

Is the Homosexual My Neighbor? A Positive Christian Response, Letha Scanzoni and Virginia R. Mollenkott. Harper San Franciso, 1994.

Pastor, I Am Gay, Rev. Howard H. Bess. Palmer Publishing Company, 1995.

Stranger at the Gate, Rev. Mel White, Simon & Schuster, 1995.

The New Testament and Homosexuality, Robin Scroggs. Augsburg Fortress, 1984.

Twice Blessed: On Being Gay & Jewish, Christie Balka and Andy Rose, Editors. Beacon Press, 1988.

What the Bible Really Says about Homosexuality, Daniel Helminiak. Alamo Square Press, 1994.

Recommended reading for gay, lesbian and bisexual people:

Becoming A Man: Half A Life Story, Paul Monette. Harper Collins, 1992.

Bi Any Other Name: Bisexual People Speak Out, Loraine Hutchins and Lani Kaahumanu, editors. Alyson Publications, 1991.

Coming Out to Parents, Mary Borhek. Pilgrim Press, 1993.

Gay Men and Women Who Enriched the World, Thomas Cowan. William Mulvey, Inc., 1988.

Hometowns: Gay Men Write About Where They Belong, John Preston, editor. Penguin, 1991.

Is It a Choice? Answers to 300 of the Most Frequently Asked Questions About Gays and Lesbians, Eric Marcus. Harper Collins, 1993.

Looking at Gay and Lesbian Life, Warren J. Blumenfeld and Diane Raymond. Beacon Press, 1988.

Outing Yourself: How to Come Out as Lesbian or Gay to Your Family, Friends, and Coworkers, Michelangelo Signorile. Random House, 1995.

Positively Gay: New Approaches to Gay and Lesbian Life, Betty Berzon, editor. Celestial Arts, 1992.

Testimonies: A Collection of Lesbian Coming Out Stories, Karen Barber and Sarah Holmes, editors. Alyson Publications, 1994.

Revelations: A Collection of Gay Male Coming Out Stories, Adrian Saks and Wayne Curtis, editors. Alyson Publications, 1994.

Uncommon Heroes: A Celebration of Heroes and Role Models for Gay and Lesbian Americans, Phillip Sherman. Fletcher Press New York, 1994.

Recommended reading for young gay, lesbian and bisexual people:

Am I Blue? Coming Out from the Silence, Marion Dane Bauer, editor. Harper Collins, 1994.

Annie On My Mind, Nancy Garden. Harper Collins, 1992.

Becoming Visible: A Reader in Gay and Lesbian History for High School and College Students, Kevin Jennings, editor. Alyson Publications, 1994.

Being Different: Lambda Youths Speak Out, Larry D. Brimmer. Grolier, 1995.

Children of the Horizons: How Gay and Lesbian Teens are Leading a New Way Out, Gilbert Herdt and Andrew Boxer. Beacon Press, 1993.

Free Your Mind: The Book for Gay and Lesbian and Bisexual Youth and Their Allies, Ellen Bass and Kate Kaufman. Harper Perennial, 1996.

Growing Up Gay/Growing Up Lesbian: A Literary Anthology, Bennett L. Singer, editor. The New Press, 1993.

Joining the Tribe: Growing Up Gay & Lesbian in the '90s, Linnea Due. Anchor Books, 1995.

The Journey Out: A Book for & About Gay, Lesbian & Bisexual Teens, Rachel Pollack and Cheryl Schwartz. Puffin Books, 1995.

Two Teenagers in Twenty, Ann Heron, editor. Alyson Publications, 1994.

Understanding Sexual Identity: A Book for Gay and Lesbian Teens, Janice Rench. Lerner, 1990.

When Someone You Know Is Gay, Susan and Daniel Cohen. Dell, 1989.

Young, Gay & Proud! Don A Romesburg, editor. Alyson Publications, 1995.

Recommended Videos:

Always My Kid: A Family Guide to Understanding Homosexuality. 1994.
74 minutes.
Triangle Video Productions, 550 Westcott, Suite 400
Houston, Texas 77007;
phone: 713-869-4477
fax: 713-861-1577

Gay Youth
Wolfe Video, P.O. Box 64
Almaden, CA 95042
phone: 408-268-6782
1-800-GET-WOLFE
website: www.wolfevideo.com

Straight From The Heart: Stories of Parents' Journeys To A New Understanding Of Their Lesbian And Gay Children. 1994, 26 minutes. Dee Mosbacher, producer.
Woman Vision Video
phone: 415-921-5678
1-800-343-5440
website: www.womanvision.org

Queer Son: Family Journeys to Understanding and Love. 1994, 48 minutes.
Vickie Seitchik
19 Jackson St.
Cape May, NJ 08204
phone: 212-929-4199

Index

INDEX

Index